# ovenly

# ovenly

SWEET & SALTY RECIPES
FROM NEW YORK'S
MOST CREATIVE BAKERY

Agatha Kulaga & Erin Patinkin

*Photography by Winona Barton-Ballentine*

Ovenly

ISBN-13: 978-0-373-89295-2

Library of Congress Cataloging-in-Publication Data

Kulaga, Agatha.

 Ovenly: sweet and salty recipes  from New York's most creative bakery / Agatha Kulaga & Erin Patinkin; photography by Winona Barton-Ballentine.

    pages cm

 Includes index.

 ISBN 978-0-373-89295-2 (alk. paper)

1. Bread. 2. Baked products. 3. Ovenly (Bakery) I. Patinkin, Erin. II. Title.

 TX769.K78 2014

 641.81'5—dc23

                                        2014005173

www.Harlequin.com

**Printed in U.S.A.**

# DEDICATION

To Chuck, Randy and Bill, for all
your guidance, support and humor.
*—Erin & Agatha*

To Phillip Kulaga and Zdzislaw Kulaga,
the two greatest men—and taste
testers—in my life. *—Agatha*

To Vanessa Selbst, for betting on
Ovenly and for taking the risk to make
a friend's dream a reality. And to Kathy,
Stuart and Dan Patinkin, for always
being there for me and for loving our
cookies so much. *—Erin*

# CONTENTS

# MY HISTORY, MY RECIPES
## *A Preface by Erin*

During my childhood in suburban Chicago, I spent countless hours in the kitchen with my grandmother and mother—Granny cooking from memory and Mom cooking mostly (and always exactly) from her massive collection of recipe clippings.

Mom wasn't one to purchase expensive hardcovers, but she did fill our home with a steady supply of cooking magazines. We had subscriptions to *Country Living*, *Cooking Light* and her favorite, *Betty Crocker*. Together, we were always trying out something new. There were a lot of successes (like the quintessentially Midwestern seven-layer cookie bar, which I remember making for the first time and still make today) and others…not so much. (I can still recall the rubbery texture and cardboard taste of a fat-free cheese and frozen-spinach casserole Mom and I whipped up during one of my parents' dieting phases.)

To my mother's credit, she also kept a trove of handwritten recipes in the drawer of a bright royal-blue kitchen wall cabinet. Each time she or my granny found success with a new dish, they would inscribe it (or, in my grandma's case, type it) twice on two separate ruled index cards—one for themselves and one for the other. The formulas came from everywhere—cooking shows, chef appearances on the local news, friends, the "old country," library books and even those *Betty Crocker* magazines. Mom and Granny communicated with each other through these recipes, and as a little kid, I tried to insert myself into that special conversation. As my brothers, Seth and Dan, intensely sorted through their respective collections of coins and baseball cards, I pawed through those recipes—picking out all the dishes I thought sounded interesting, narrowing them down into a small stack, and running to my mom when I found something particularly good. That small stuffed cabinet drawer was the treasure chest of my childhood, full of unexplored possibilities.

My mom continues this handwritten tradition: almost weekly I receive a magazine clipping or a neatly printed three-by-five card, reliably accompanied by brief messages in her perfect schoolteacher script. "There's dark chocolate in this recipe. You love that!" or "I made this last weekend. Delicious! Dad says you have to make it at Ovenly!" or "I ripped this out of a *Bon Appétit* sitting in the doctor's office. Don't tell anyone!" I add those recipes to my own kitchen cabinet drawer of culinary wonders.

When Granny passed away and I inherited her painstakingly organized recipes, I discovered that she was trading not only with her daughter, but also with her close circle of chatty and boisterous lady friends. There were article clippings from magazines and newspapers, including ones featuring "Nancy Reagan's Famous Brownies"; banquet-size (and outdated dishes) like chicken à la king for one hundred people; and instructions on how to make walnut *kiffel,* with additional notes written in some blend of English, Hungarian and German. Granny's cards were not just about the food of a certain time, but also about relationships, culture and tradition. They are a homemade slice of my grandma's rich history, and a way for me to keep her with me always.

One of Granny's recipe boxes sits next to me as I type this preface, the words Menu Maker pressed into the green plastic lid. As I rummage through her cards for the millionth time, I vividly recall the tang and crunchiness of the broiled pimento-olive toast that she (and Mom) made for every social gathering, the feeling of her pineapple cheesecake melting on my tongue—fluffy and sweet—and the buttery flakiness of her apricot *kolacky,* dusted with confectioners' sugar. These cards—along with my own collection of handwritten notes, cookbook scribbles and magazine clippings, and my "Recipes to Try" digital folder that I share with Agatha—are more than a collection of weights and measurements and oven temperatures. They are a chronicle of the flavors of my youth. I can tie each of those delicious recollections to those sweet and savory moments of my own slices of history...my middle school graduation, a road trip to a Phish concert (yes, I was that teenager), the first time I made a boy dinner and the family gathering following my granny's funeral.

Unlike my inheritance of handwritten gems, the first cookbook I ever owned was, in appearance, unremarkable. It was a thin publication with four-color photos titled something like *Oriental Cuisine,* sold alongside woks and rice steamers in a now closed department store whose name I can't recall. When we were only seven or eight years old, my brother Dan (just a year and a half my senior) and I were totally obsessed with Martin Yan's long-running PBS series, *Yan Can Cook.* During each beloved episode, I would imagine that I was Chef Yan's sous-chef—expertly smashing make-believe garlic cloves into a gooey paste with my pretend Ginsu knife, and deftly chopping the tails off of phantom shrimp with a swiftness and dexterity that I have never actually possessed. (I'm a total klutz. Ask Agatha about the time I spilled ten pounds of tiny flaxseeds all over her kitchen floor or when I burned my entire right hand with boiling sticky caramel.) My mother rewarded my enthusiasm for Mr. Yan's Chinese dishes with both the Chinese cookbook and a shiny new wok. (Dan probably got a new Transformers or Walter Payton T-shirt.) I was pumped.

Properly equipped, I began my first independent culinary experiment: beef stir-fry. Though my mom supervised—cutting things when they needed to be cut, watching closely as I coated meat in corn starch for frying, and reminding me to be careful as I steamed the rice on the stove while standing on a stool—she let me make the meal almost entirely on my own. When dinner was ready, I served it to my family and eagerly watched them clean their plates and then ask for seconds. Dan and Seth likely emitted some sort of gastric approval. They liked it! My confidence grew as I tinkered more and more, and as I did, I became more and more food obsessed. A wacky quality for a kid in the 1980s.

Those were the days when being a "foodie" wasn't a pop culture thing. While my brothers were playing T-ball down the street or practicing WWF-inspired wrestling moves on one another, and my girlfriends were making up dances to the newest New Kids on the Block videos (I thought Joey McIntyre was just the dreamiest, but second only to my inexplicable childhood crush on Rod Stewart), my idea of a good time was hovering around my friends' kitchens. Across the tracks at Sarah Gorajski's house, I pestered her father for tips as he prepared deep-fried soft-shell crabs. A few more blocks away, at Dana Lord's house, I taste tested her mom's *scharole*—a spicy, brothy and herby escarole soup—and came home begging my mom to call Dana's mother so we could make it on our own. And my favorite was going to Granny's to help bake yellow cake with chocolate icing, date cookies or Chocolate Cheesecake with Sour Cream Topping (see recipe on page 153).

As I matured, so did my palate and my sweet tooth. When I was a preteen, I experimented with creating the perfect brownie (my strategy was to use as much chocolate and butter as possible). When I became a vegetarian in high school, I paged through Mollie Katzen's *Moosewood Cookbook* so often that the cover fell off. (That book was the inspiration for Ovenly's Whole Wheat Banana Bread [see recipe on page 53]). At the University of Wisconsin, you could find me on Library Mall, reading about perfect pie crusts à la Rose Levy Beranbaum (whose recipe served as muse for our Pâte Brisée pastry dough [see recipe on page 98]). Even as I was busy pursuing my master's in arts management, I was challenging myself to concoct the best possible vegan chocolate chip cookie (see recipe on page 77), which, oddly enough, ended up being the world's *perfect* chocolate chip cookie. Period.

But at the age of twenty-six, I had not yet ventured into food as a real profession. At some point, I had deliberated about going to pastry school and had dabbled in blog writing, but I felt pressured to pursue a more "traditional" career, so I entered a graduate program instead. Once I finished, I continued to eschew any culinary aspirations and found a safe and secure position as the executive director of a small nonprofit arts center near Chicago—the perfect job for someone my age with my degree. But my heart wasn't in it, and it wasn't long before I was bored out of my mind and relegated to only dreaming of being a chef.

Finally, one night after a gridlocked commute home from work on the Eisenhower Expressway, I pulled out that "Menu Maker" box one more time. I reached for it to look for dessert inspiration, but looking back, I think I was searching for answers to the questions, What should I do with my life, and what will make me happy? A lightbulb went off.

We've heard it said a million times that "you are what you eat." But right then I had the epiphany that *I am what I cook*. My one true, indefatigable passion was cooking and baking. More than from anything else, I found joy in my creative experiences in the kitchen, from the pleasure on friends' faces when I fed them a yummy meal, from the miraculous metamorphosis of a few simple ingredients into something beautiful, shareable and delicious. I was suffering behind my desk. I had to change the status quo.

The transition wasn't swift by any means. For months, I hemmed and hawed as I gathered the courage to bid farewell to my go-getting job, to my boyfriend and dear friends, to my family and the Midwestern culture and geography that had swaddled and shaped me. Saying goodbye was scary, but I had to let go of all that was familiar in order to say hello to the gritty, chaotic, thrilling and inspiring test kitchen that is New York City. Here, I finally took the risk to embrace my dreams.

Though I would not meet Agatha for another two years, and though Ovenly would not come to be for another three, the move motivated me, and I seriously began to hash out business ideas (and I had about a million of them). Culinary tinkerers—bloggers like Deb Perelman, professionally trained chefs like Claudia Fleming, TV personalities like Martin Yan and especially home cooks like Mom and Granny—were my inspiration. They were funny, thorough, smart, demanding and always encouraging. They fueled my passion, gave me opportunities to experiment, and ultimately provided me with the courage to take a risk and pursue my true love. They were my teachers. Ovenly and this book have come to be largely because of them.

I hope, if anything, that in writing this book, Agatha and I provide some of the same inspiration for you. And, please, feel free to write our recipes down on index cards and send them on to your loved ones. We would be honored.

## Filled Walnut Kiffel (Nut Roll)

1½ cups (3/4#) Fresh Butter    4 to 6 cups flour (1#)
1 cake yeast    1/2 cup sugar
1 teaspoon vanilla    1/2 cup cream or milk
5 eggs separated

Add to beaten egg yolks the sugar, vanilla and 1/2 of the
cream. Dissolve the yeast with the rest of the cream
(lukewarm). Add a little flour, let stand and raise.
Rub the butter into the rest of the flour. Combine the
mixtures. Add more flour if necessary. Roll the dough
quite thin, cut into small squares. Place a portion of
the filling in each square, beginning at one corner and
form into crescent shape. Place in pan and frost with
the beaten whites of 5 eggs, let rise 2 or more hours
covered with towel. Bake 30 Min in moderate oven at 350
                                     (over)

---

## DIVINITY PUFFS

2½ cups sugar
1/2 cup white corn syrup
1/2 cup

1/2 teaspoon vani
1/2 cup chopped,
   or red can ed
   cherries

whites
and water to thin-syrup s
egg whites, beating co
to thread stage (23
   beating constantly.
ge (248°); add

---

## Great Cheese cake

Crust - 1 cup sifted enriched flour
   1/4 cup sugar
   1/2 teaspoon grated lemon peel
   1/2 cup butter or margerine
   1 slightly beaten egg yolk
   1/4 teaspoon vanilla

Combine flour, sugar and lemon peel.
Cut in butter till crumbly. Add egg yolk and vanilla. Blend thoroughly. (Pat 1/3 of the dough on bottom of 9" spring-form pan
(sides removed) bake in hot oven 400" about 6 minutes or
till golden. Cool. butter sides of pan and attach to a height
Pat remaining dough evenly on sides to a height

---

## RAINBOW CAKE

1 sm pkg - strawberry- lime-lemon-orange jello
4 small cans milnot chilled
Dissolve each pkg of jello in 1 cup boiling
water- let cool until mixture just starte
set (not stiff) Beat one can milno
(until stiff) add one fl
into slightly oi

---

1 teaspoon a
Combine water, sugar, salt, c
and shortening; cook 3 minutes. Cool to luke
Soften yeast in this mixture. Add flour; mix
soft dough. Let rise about 1½ hours. Add
flour to make a stiff dough; knead lightly.
in greased bowl; cover with damp clot
rise until doubled in bulk, about 2 hours.
2 portions. Cover and let ris

---

Mix sugar and milk and cook, stirri
or until a little of the mixtur
dropped into cold water. Set
vanilla and salt. B
Beat until
buttered pa
into each pi

---

brown sugar
1 tablesp
1 teaspoon

ut meats

3 cup G
melted
8 minute

---

GOLD CUPCAR

1/2 cup shortening
1 cup sugar
ten egg yolks
n baking powder
ortening thoroughly,
A - add sifted dry in
put in greased pans

---

oleo
2 tbl
13x9
ingredi
et aside
water
peed
ream

up salad oil
baking soda
chopped walnuts

atter will be thick
floured oblong pan.

lsp soft oleo
tsp vanilla
on cake.

---

2 cups sugar
2 cups flour
1 tsp Baking P
1 can crushed
Mix Pour into
   teaspoon baking powder
1/4 cu

# A REFUGE IN THE KITCHEN

*A Preface by Agatha*

As the daughter of two Polish immigrants who met in a small industrial city in Connecticut, I was raised bilingual, speaking Polish at home and English everywhere else. My family ate traditional Eastern European dishes, including liverwurst, headcheese and tripe, at every meal. Believe it or not, I loved it all.

My parents were quite cunning; they never told me what these foods actually were until I was already hooked, thus inadvertently (or deliberately) raising me to be an adventurous eater from the time I was tiny. Thanks to their dinner table sleight of hand, I proudly enjoy those foods to this day. Not many people in the world can claim to be a headcheese aficionado.

Aside from consuming the neglected parts of farm animals, some of my fondest memories of food go back to weekend visits to my *babcia's* house in New Haven, Connecticut. It was a quiet forty-five-minute drive there from our house, but it always felt like an eternity. She maintained a giant, messy garden that mesmerized me. Each visit, immediately upon arrival, I would dive right into the tangled green mess, in search of edible treasures. A short time later, I would emerge bare bellied with a stretched-out T-shirt full of juicy strawberries, perfectly ripe gooseberries and tart red currants, which I loved to pinch until they popped. Whatever fruit I could resist eating went into the sweets we baked that day. Currants have held a special place in my heart since then and eventually became the inspiration for Ovenly's Currant Rosemary Scones (see recipe on page 31).

I never ceased to be amazed by the sheer volume of desserts that my grandmother was capable of whipping up in a day's time. She baked for any occasion or no occasion at all. Her table was permanently set with my favorites: airy cake layered with dense, wet poppy seeds; lightly fried *pączki* filled with homemade prune jam; and a simple buttery apple cake (all of which have inspired our coffee cake variations [see recipe on page 43]). At first glance, it always seemed to be an insurmountable feast. Yet my family and I always found a way to devour every last morsel, often when a dish was still steaming from the oven. I suspect that this was around the time I developed the bad habit of tasting baked goods straight out of the oven and still blazing hot; my stomach is grateful, but my tongue has repeatedly suffered the consequences.

Though my grandmother's kitchen barely fit the two of us at one time, she always invited me to squeeze in next to her. Her stoic nature left no room for small talk, only concentrated yet seemingly effortless work. Her hands moved quickly and rhythmically. I studied her, carefully counting the number of times she stirred a batter, analyzing the pressure and method she used to pat down a mound of sticky, wet dough, or her technique for cracking an egg. I don't remember seeing any recipes or proper measuring tools; everything was measured by eye and recalled from memory. This was how I learned my first recipes—by memorizing them, never writing them down.

During my childhood, my mother's mental health deteriorated. After years of struggle, my parents eventually separated and my father bravely took on the role of sole caretaker of my younger brother and me. I don't think my father had much choice at the time, but he did so without any hesitation, for which I will always be grateful. So at fourteen, I became the woman of the house. I gave up, at least partially, my short-lived career as a boy-crazy teenager and assumed adult responsibilities, like bossing my brother around, organizing our spice cabinets and attempting to re-create meals that I had watched my parents make when I was younger. Rushing home from school to prepare "gourmet" family dinners before my dad got home from work was exhilarating. Soon I began to fancy myself a chef.

In those days, the base ingredients for most of our meals were chicken and potatoes (which explains my aversion to potatoes to this day). However, the preparation methods and flavor combinations were without limits. The meat mallet was my favorite, maybe because it allowed me to release some teenage angst. I loved playing with different spices and fresh herbs (and I still do today). I realized early on that butter was my secret weapon: it made everything taste better. I'm sure I subjected our family to some terrible meals, but I'll never know. My father's gleaming look of appreciation for and approval of every meal will forever be embedded in my memory, and it is what inspired me to continue my experimentation in the kitchen.

Throughout high school and college, I developed a serious obsession with science (yes, I was a science geek). However, in between reading about neuropsychology and rehabilitative medicine, I spent most of my waking moments waiting tables in unexceptional yet notoriously busy Boston restaurants. While my duties were always in the front of the house, I often lurked near the hot kitchen with the cooks. I wanted to understand how the food I was serving had actually come to life. Plus, I loved being in the company of the cooks, who were generally foulmouthed and hilarious badasses.

In 2001 I packed my bags and left Boston for New York City to put my recently completed psychology degree into practice. One month after I arrived, the Twin Towers fell. In the weeks following 9/11, it became not only impossible to find a job, but also inappropriate to even inquire about one. Unexpectedly, I found myself with an abundance of invaluable free time on my hands. So I holed up in my kitchen with the only two cookbooks I owned, the *Joy of Cooking* and Harold McGee's *On Food and Cooking,* and began to bake ferociously.

Eventually, and miraculously, I was hired by a mental health and addictions program at a New York University hospital, where I would later become a clinical director and assistant professor. Something about taking the job felt predestined, given the circumstances of my childhood. This would be the place where I would both begin and end my career in psychology. It was gratifying to know that during my time there, I was instrumental in helping people make positive changes in their lives. But after ten years of listening to their stories, I felt emotionally sapped.

After plenty of personal and professional exposure to chaos and stress, my soul needed restoration, and I found refuge in the comfort and precision of baking. When I frosted a cake or inhaled the scent of bread rising, all felt right with the world. My knack for using simple ingredients inventively came naturally. It was all I knew, and it would turn out to be a great gift.

I had believed I was happy and satisfied with my career, but the purest contentment and satisfaction I felt was in the kitchen. The idea to start a food business was tucked in the back of my mind somewhere, but I never paid it much attention. It was too intimidating to think about doing it alone, and it was much easier to ignore the desire—until I met Erin.

We met at a Four Burners meeting, a food-focused book club founded by my childhood friend Cara Cannella. That meeting changed everything—and quickly. Erin and I immediately began discussing our mutual desire to work with food. Within a week we had made so much progress that starting a business together actually became a clear and realistic objective. Though I had just met her, I knew that Erin would be the perfect partner in crime. It might have been her unruly curls and fierce attitude that first caught my attention, but I like to think we wore our mutual determination, obsession with food and Eastern European work ethic on our sleeves. That first auspicious meeting led to the birth of Ovenly.

My early memories of food helped shape my palate and inspired my culinary exploration of Greenpoint, a predominantly Polish neighborhood in Brooklyn, where I would eventually settle down. This small community, which is now also home to Ovenly's flagship location, became the quiet cultural backdrop for my continued exploration of all things sweet and savory. In the spirit of M. F. K. Fisher, who saw "food as something beautiful to be shared with people instead of as a thrice-daily necessity," I hope that this cookbook inspires you to see the beauty in food, and in our recipes, and to share those experiences with everyone you love.

# INTRODUCTION

We strained to open our eyes. They were sealed shut from a puffiness that came with months of sleep deprivation. Or maybe it was from the cold and damp air of an early spring morning. The windows of Wedgie, our rusty 1998 Ford Explorer–cum–delivery car, were fogged from the warmth of our breath.

After our morning deliveries we were so tired that we had found a parking spot on a dark, desolate street near our former commercial kitchen in industrial Red Hook, Brooklyn, and had taken a nap. Now we were cursing ourselves. The sun was up, and we had passed out for way longer than the hour we had allotted. There was still so much baking to do! We rubbed our bloodshot eyes and stretched to work the kinks out of our weary limbs. It was time to start the day.

Back then, sleeping in Wedgie was par for the course. We had quit our jobs to pursue Ovenly full-time, and as nascent entrepreneurs, we did everything ourselves—we baked, we washed the dishes, we made the deliveries, we kept the books and we maintained the inventory. Our day started at 3:00 a.m. and ended around midnight, if at all. Looking back, it's hard to believe how far we've come (although we admit that we sometimes still nap in strange places).

We launched Ovenly in September 2010. Over a year before, we found ourselves gathered around Erin's dining room table, munching on insanely good Pistachio Cardamom Cupcakes with Dark Chocolate Ganache (Agatha's; see recipe on page 151). The two of us were part of a food-focused book club, and though we had each been in the group for many months, we had never seemed to attend the same meetings, but we had heard about one another from other members. Then, in late April 2009, we finally found ourselves in a room together.

We were supposed to discuss a book on the evolution of Indian cuisine, but after a few glasses of wine, the intellectual conversation quickly died. Instead we found ourselves talking about our favorite new restaurants, cocktails and cookbooks. But when Erin floated the idea that the group was ripe for an entrepreneurial venture, the conversation quickly turned into a one-on-one between the two of us. That night, we decided to set up a time to talk seriously (and soberly).

Looking back, it was partnership at first sight.

On May 2, 2009, we met at Colson Patisserie in Park Slope. Erin showed up late and groggy. Agatha was early and perfectly coiffed, with pen and notebook in hand. Despite our different takes on first impressions and timeliness, we discovered we were at very similar points in our lives: nearing thirty, feeling complacent in our careers and wanting to turn our shared passion for baking into something more than a hobby.

After that, we spent many hours together. We'd hole up in our apartments—testing ideas, swapping recipes, teaching each other tricks and chatting long past midnight. As time wore on, we discovered that our differences and similarities made us a very yin-yang pair: Our shared Eastern European heritage had fomented our lifelong love of cooking and eating. Experimenting and perfecting our own recipes was our favorite pastime. Agatha's salty-foods addiction and knack for details played nicely against Erin's insatiable sweet tooth and big-picture thinking. We both loved blasting R. Kelly while experimenting in the kitchen. You get the idea.

From that first meeting until today, Ovenly's growth charts a journey that began with making deliveries on foot, walking sheets of still-warm scones from our apartments to neighborhood cafés, and continues into the present, where a typical day involves serving hundreds at our flagship shop at 31 Greenpoint Avenue in Brooklyn, overseeing daily deliveries to clients from Philadelphia to Upstate New York, and shipping loads of gift boxes to customers across the country. Along the way, we've faced plenty of (now entertaining) setbacks—like six failed weeks spent trying to make an Ovenly version of Combos (one day we will conquer you, homemade Combos!) and the time the refrigerator and sink from our commercial kitchen simply vanished in the middle of the night (yep, that happened). Now we're lucky enough to work with an amazing team of bakers and even have a proper delivery van (RIP, Wedgie) manned by official drivers. We may be off the road ourselves these days, but we're still in front of the oven—baking, testing, tweaking and tasting.

As a creative kitchen that specializes in sweets and snacks, we aim to make innovative treats that surprise and delight the palate with unexpected flavor combinations (think molasses cookies accented by whole grain mustard [see recipe on page 80], or shortbread spiced up with black caraway and smoked sea salt [see recipe on page 88]). Sometimes we play on tradition—our ginger sesame corn is like Cracker Jack for adults—and we tend to test the limits of indulgence (bacon and butter, anyone?). For us, the definition of delicious is a balance of savory and sweet with just the right hint of spice, and we've spent years perfecting these recipes.

In the Ovenly kitchen, we make everything from what you crave when you first roll out of bed (buttery scones, fresh muffins and savory tarts), to your ultimate pleasures (chewy cookies, dense, crumbly shortbreads and rich layered cakes), to what you hunger for after a few rounds (smoky, beer-slicked caramel corn; bacony peanuts; and spicy-sweet bar mixes). Back when our flavor panelists were limited to boyfriends, roommates, friends and family members, we could have never imagined that our fans would one day span the country, that our little Greenpoint shop would be flooded with customers from the moment we opened in May 2012, or that we'd be voted best new bakery in New York City soon after.

No matter who happens to be scarfing down our treats, we tend to hear this common refrain: "What the *#$&!!! is *in* this! Crack?" We are happy to report that our secret is not illegal substances. In fact, our recipes are friendly, simple and definitely won't get you thrown behind bars. Though, if you want them to be perfect, buy the primo stuff: we recommend bacon from Benton's, chocolate from Guittard or Callebaut or any of your bean-to-bar favorites, beer from Brooklyn Brewery and local dairy (in our case, from Battenkill Valley Creamery).

*Ovenly* is packed with all our greatest hits—herby-sweet scones, the best chocolate chip cookies you've ever tasted and insanely addictive caramel corn—plus tons of pages devoted to recipe riffs and spin-offs. As self-taught, curious cooks, we hope to offer readers a straight-talking approach that is never too fussy and always encourages experimentation. Hopefully, the tips and tricks we've developed and refined over the past few years will make your baking journey as fun for you as ours has been for us.

Above all, we believe that cooking (and eating!) should be an adventure—and that is the guiding spirit of this book and, frankly, of everything we do. For both of us, our most fulfilling moments have always been centered around cooking and eating. Our hope is that through this cookbook we will share that part of ourselves with you— and offer up the pure pleasure that comes from creating and savoring this food.

# ESSENTIAL TOOLS & INGREDIENTS

This chapter is a pared-down guide to our baking and snack nomenclature, and to the necessities you'll need to accomplish the recipes in this book. Included here are facts, tips, tricks, not-so-common ingredients and equipment. This guide is not a list of every single process or ingredient you will find in this book; it's just a summary of the less common or more essential ones. We have written this book with the assumption that the home baker has a general knowledge of basic tools and ingredients.

# ESSENTIAL TOOLS

### Bench Scraper

A bench scraper is indispensable for scraping surfaces; for turning pâte brisée and other butter doughs while rolling; for transferring ingredients, such as chopped chocolate, from a cutting board to a bowl (or other cooking apparatus); and for cutting brownies, bars and coffee cakes.

### Cardboard Rounds

Precut corrugated cardboard rounds are precise in shape and totally necessary when decorating cakes. Hidden by the frosting, these rounds help to keep cakes sturdy and allow them to be transported more easily. Rounds can be purchased at kitchenware or craft stores or online.

### Digital Scale

For dedicated home bakers, and for professional ones like us, a scale provides the most accurate measurements for consistency.

### Dry & Liquid Measuring Cups

As their names imply, dry measuring cups are for measuring dry ingredients (flours, nuts, seeds, cocoa), while liquid measuring cups are for measuring wet ingredients (oils, water, dairy products). Use a spoon to transfer ingredients to your dry measures, fill them completely and use a knife or bench scraper to level them off. Liquid measures feature gradations (usually in cups and milliliters) and include a pour spout for easy usage.

Why not just use one or the other, you ask? Liquid measures are generally accurate within a fraction of an ounce, no matter the liquid. For example, 8 ounces (1 cup) of olive oil is going to be generally equal to a cup of buttermilk.

This does not hold true for dry measures, since dry ingredients settle and have different masses. For example, a cup of flour may weigh much more than a cup of oats or dried cherries. For our cookbook, we've chosen to measure in cups, taking into account the weight differences of different types of ingredients, so using the right measuring tools is important when preparing an Ovenly recipe.

### Offset Spatula

Offset spatulas are integral in frosting cakes (see process on page 146–147), great for cupcake frosting details, perfect for smoothing out batters in pans and much more.

### Oven Thermometer

Don't let your oven temperature display or dial fool you—ovens vary in temperature, despite what your digital screen or dial may tell you. We always use an oven thermometer to ensure baking accuracy, and we suggest you do, too.

### Paper or Silicone Baking Cups

These allow for the easy removal of muffins and cupcakes from the pan, prevent sticking and make cleaning up much easier. We prefer to use unbleached baking cups, such as those from Beyond Gourmet.

### Pastry Bags & Tips

For executing cake details and frosting perfect cupcakes, we suggest investing a few dollars in a reusable pastry bag and a variety of tip sizes and shapes. If you are a novice cake decorator, we recommend purchasing size 14, 18 and 22 open star tips and size 2, 4 and 6 plain/round tips to start or a basic cake-decorating kit, such as Wilton's 12-piece cupcake decorating set (widely available at craft stores or online).

### Revolving Cake Stand

If you get into cake decorating, a revolving cake stand (like a lazy Susan) will make your life much easier. A revolving cake stand allows you to spin your cake while you frost, and it helps you to determine whether you have decorated a cake evenly and perfectly. We prefer models with a heavy cast-iron base (like those by Ateco), but plastic works, too. These are widely available in kitchenware stores or online.

### Rimmed Sheet Pans & Baking Pans

We prefer uncoated, rimmed, steel or aluminum half-sheet (18 x 13-inch) and quarter-sheet (9 x 13-inch) pans (also known as rimmed sheet pans) for home use. They are ideal for baking cookies, rolling shortbread and roasting nuts and seeds. Sheet pans of various sizes are widely available at kitchenware stores or online.

When we refer to a baking pan, we recommend using one that is at least 2 inches deep. Our standard baking pans are 9 x 9 inches or 9 x 13 inches.

### Ruler

To create a lattice pie crust, evenly sized Hot Tarts or perfectly square bars, we recommend using a dedicated metal kitchen ruler. It will make cutting easier and will make your pastry look perfect.

## Scoops

For us, scoops are essential in cookie making. Using a scoop ensures that each cookie is the same size and, therefore, that each bakes evenly. Scoops come in a variety of sizes, but we recommend purchasing one #20 scoop (1⅝ ounces) for larger cookies and one #30 (1 ounce) for smaller cookies.

## Stand Mixers & Hand Mixers

While we acknowledge that stand mixers are an investment, they are worth it. Well built and powerful, stand mixers are long-lasting and great for aerating batters, whipping creams and more. They are also very useful in savory cooking and bread making.

If you do not have a stand mixer, a hand mixer can be used to make recipes that call for a stand mixer. However, hand mixers generally are not as powerful; in recipes that call for aeration or whipping, or to fully incorporate some of our thicker cookie batters, you may have to add a minute or so to your mixing time.

# CHOOSING A BAKING PAN

A pan's color and material will affect baking times and temperatures. Different materials—glass, dark nonstick, aluminum and stainless steel—conduct heat differently. For our recipes, we bake everything on light-colored stainless-steel or aluminum pans. If that is what you are baking with, then do not feel the need to adjust the recipe.

Dark pans (dark gray nonstick, for example) absorb heat more quickly than light-colored metal pans, which causes crusts to brown more quickly. This increases the possibility for a pastry to crisp on the outside without fully baking on the inside. If you have only dark pans available, lower the oven temperature by 25°F. The baking time may also need adjusting.

Like dark pans, glass cookware heats up very quickly. When using clear glass, reduce the oven temperature by 25°F and test your pastries with a toothpick to avoid burning or undercooking the centers.

# MARKING PANS & CREATING GRIDS FOR CUTTING BROWNIES, BARS & SHORTBREADS

Marking an aluminum or steel baking pan with filed scratch marks will make cutting brownies, bars and shortbreads easy and precise.

Tools Needed: permanent marker like a fine point Sharpie, half-round metal file, one 9 x 13-inch rimmed aluminum sheet pan, inflexible 18-inch steel ruler or a yardstick, offset spatula

Using your marker or Sharpie, make a mark every 3 inches on both short (9-inch) sides of the sheet pan (you will make 2 marks on each side). Then make a mark every 3¼ inches on both long (13-inch) sides (you will make 3 marks on each side). With the edge of your metal file, make a $\frac{1}{16}$-inch file mark over the Sharpie marks.

If you are scoring before baking (shortbreads only), once your pan is filled with batter, use your ruler to connect opposing file marks. Hold the ruler steady and run your knife along the top of your batter,

making scores for 12 bars. Remove the ruler and cut the score marks all the way through. Use an offset spatula to remove the batter from the pan and then place on a parchment-lined rimmed sheet pan before baking (or freezing).

If you are scoring after baking (brownies and bars), cool your treats completely before scoring and cutting as above. Use an offset spatula to remove your brownies or bars from the pan.

*Tip*

*You can make your brownies, bars and shortbreads any size you like! Just make even measurements and mark your pans wherever you please.*

# ESSENTIAL INGREDIENTS

## Baking Powder

Baking powder is a combination of baking soda and an acidic salt, such as cream of tartar, plus cornstarch. Like baking soda, baking powder is a chemical leavening agent that causes batters to rise when they are baked. Combined with baking soda, baking powder does most of the leavening, while the baking soda neutralizes the acids found in the powder.

Too much baking powder can produce bitter batter. It also can make a batter rise too rapidly, creating large air bubbles, which may cause the batter to break and fall. If you use too little baking powder, your baked goods may be dense. For this reason, when you are creating your own recipes, be mindful of *how* you use baking powder and *how much* you use in a recipe.

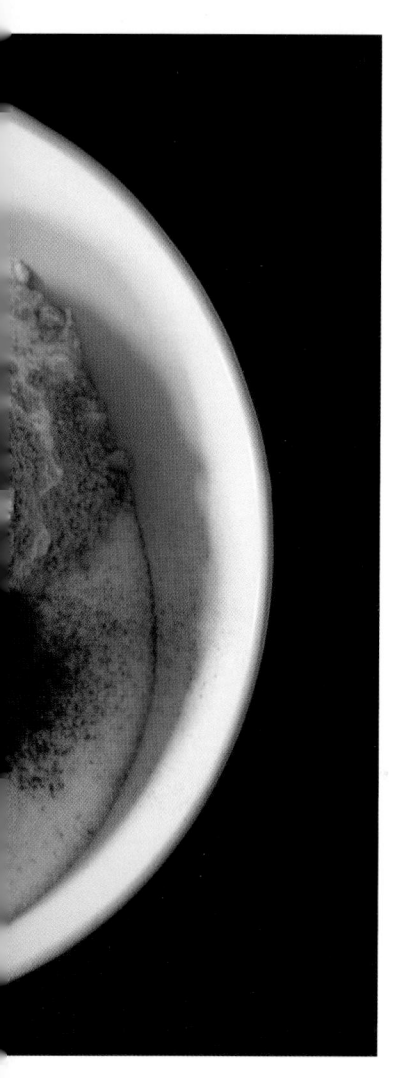

### Baking Soda

Baking soda (sodium bicarbonate) is a leavening agent. When combined with an acid (like that found in baking powder, yogurt, lemons and more), it releases carbon dioxide, which makes batters expand and rise.

### Butter

When we specify butter at room temperature (about 65°F), we mean just that. For recipes that call for mixing and creaming butter, the butter should be cool to the touch and easily retain your fingerprint when you touch it. Butter that is too soft (over 68°F), melted butter, or butter that has been melted and then cooled, should not be used in recipes that require creaming.

We use unsalted Grade A butter (preferably local) in our recipes. The fresher the butter and the higher its quality, the better tasting your baked goods and pastries will be. If you don't plan on using butter right away, freeze it to preserve its flavor.

### Cardamom

We prefer to buy whole green cardamom pods and to grind them ourselves. Grind whole pods in a coffee or spice grinder until a fine powder forms. Remove any fibrous strands before using.

### Chocolate

The general rule of thumb is buy the best chocolate you can afford, and one that has the fewest ingredients. Brands we love include Callebaut, Guittard, Scharffen Berger, Taza and Valrhona. For most recipes, unless otherwise noted, we recommend using chocolate with a 60 percent cocoa content or higher. The higher the percentage of cocoa, the darker—and the less sweet and more bitter—the chocolate will be.

If you are vegan, for our chocolate chip cookie recipe, be sure to use a chocolate that does not contain milk or milk solids (most high-quality dark and bittersweet chocolates do not contain dairy products).

### Dark Dutch–Process Cocoa Powder

Dark Dutch-process cocoa powder (also called extra dark, black, black onyx and cocoa noir) has a high alkali content, a low fat content, an intense bittersweet chocolate flavor and a beautiful black hue. This cocoa powder is essential to our Brooklyn Blackout Cake (see recipe on page 142) and our Salted Dark Chocolate Pudding (see recipe on page 184). Since dark Dutch-process cocoa powder can dry out cookies and other baked goods, be sure to use it in very wet doughs and in small amounts in other cookery.

This cocoa powder is available by special order from Sahadi's (www.sahadis.com) and Surfas Culinary District (www.culinarydistrict.com).

## Dutch-Process Cocoa Powder vs. American-Process (Natural)

Dutch-process cocoa powder has been alkalized to make it neutral, and it will not react with leavening agents. American-process (natural) cocoa powder is acidic and, therefore, will react with and activate leavening agents (baking soda, baking powder and so on).

Generally, American-process cocoa powders are sharper, smokier and more acidic than Dutch-process cocoa powders, which are deeper and have a purer chocolate flavor. For the most part, our recipes do not rely on cocoa powders to enhance the rising power of leavening agents, so you can use American-process and Dutch-process cocoa powders interchangeably. The key is to buy high-quality cocoa, like Guittard or Scharffen Berger.

## Eggs

Eggs come in a few different sizes (large, extra-large and so on). We use large eggs in all our recipes. A general rule is to bake with eggs that are at room temperature. At room temperature, eggs and dairy products combine to form a bond that traps air. When batters and doughs are heated, the air expands, producing a lighter crumb. For this reason, we also like to let our milk and cream come to room temperature before baking, unless otherwise noted.

### Testing Eggs for Freshness

We prefer local eggs from pasture-raised hens. Since these often don't have an expiration date on them, stick any questionable whole eggs in a bowl of water to determine their freshness. Fresh eggs will sink, and rotten eggs will float. So if any of your eggs float, throw them out.

### Separating Eggs

Crack the egg on the side of a bowl, pry the shell open and let the whites run out until all that remains is the yolk. Or crack the egg on a flat surface, dump the egg into the palm of your hand and let the whites run through your fingers until all that's left is the yolk.

## Jam

We prefer to make our own (see recipe on page 193), but if you use store-bought, be sure to reduce the jam (or jelly or marmalade) before using it in a recipe, such as in our holiday cookies. To do so, bring the jam to a boil in a saucepan, and then simmer it for 5 minutes to thicken it. Let it cool before using.

## Milk, Cream & Buttermilk

### Milk

In all our recipes that call for milk, use whole milk. Whole milk contains about 3.5 percent fat, and as you would guess, 2 percent milk has that exact fat content and skim contains none. Fat helps bind ingredients together and will help your baked goods and pastries come out tender and moist.

### Heavy Cream vs. Whipping Cream

Heavy cream and whipping cream differ in that the former contains at least 36 percent milk fat and the latter contains at least 30 percent. For our recipes, you can use either type. For recipes that call for whipped cream or for whipping cream until it is stiff, the more fat, the more stable it will be. We recommend using heavy cream (the cream with the higher fat content) for piping decorations, frostings and whipped toppings.

### Buttermilk

Buttermilk adds a rich tang and moisture to many of our recipes. We believe in using the real stuff, full fat, if you can find it. If not, widely available low-fat buttermilk will do.

## Natural Food Coloring

We use only natural food coloring for our red velvet cake and our Pomegranate Buttercream (see recipe on page 182). The artificial stuff is a derivative of coal tar and petroleum, so we avoid it. Natural food coloring from India Tree and Chef Master Naturals are largely available in health food stores or online.

## Nuts & Seeds

As with spices, the fresher nuts and seeds are, the better. Since nuts and seeds are high in fat, they can go rancid. To prevent rancidity, we keep ours in an airtight container in the freezer (which also preserves their flavor better than the refrigerator) if we won't be using them right away. Experiment by substituting your favorite nuts and seeds in any of our recipes that call for them.

## Oats

We use rolled oats (not quick-cooking oats) in our recipes. Rolled oats and gluten-free rolled oats differ only in the fact that the latter is milled in a gluten-free certified facility. If you don't have a gluten sensitivity, feel free to use regular oats.

## Organic vs. Local

Local ingredients found at markets or in specialty grocery stores create a lower carbon footprint and—especially if purchased at a farmers' market or directly from a farmer—tend to be fresher. As we've said, in both baking and cooking, the fresher the ingredients, the better. When locally grown ingredients are not available, we try to use organic ones wherever we can. Organic ingredients are now widely available in local grocery stores.

## Pomegranate Molasses

One of our favorite ingredients, pomegranate molasses lends a bright, tart and fruity flavor to cakes and frostings (and it's all natural!). When not using it in one of the recipes, try it in a cocktail. Pomegranate molasses is available from most Middle Eastern specialty stores, or online.

## Salts

Part of the fun with many of our recipes is choosing which salt to finish cookies and bars. For crunch, we usually reach for a coarse-grained sea salt like La Baleine or a flaked sea salt like Maldon for its beauty and sheen. Light pink Himalayan salt and black volcanic salt are also great for decoration and flavor.

These salts are widely available in stores or online.

## Spices

Use dried spices that are as fresh as possible, as they lose their potency over time. We purchase the majority of our spices for home use from The Spice House in Chicago (www.thespicehouse.com). We love the quality of their products.

## Vanilla Beans

To remove the tiny vanilla "caviar" from their tough skins, slice a vanilla bean length-wise. Then, using the edge of the knife, scrape the caviar from the entire pod. Tap the seeds into a bowl or directly into your mixture. Stuff any used pods into your sugar jar. Just a few will flavor the sugar, which is great for baking, poaching fruits and more.

## Vanilla Extract

Vanilla extract is made from preserving vanilla beans in alcohol. Be sure to use only the pure stuff (not imitation). Vanilla extract is also very easy to make: Simply slice three vanilla beans lengthwise, and place them in a pint-size jar with an airtight lid. Add a cup of your favorite booze (we personally like using bourbon, the cheap stuff), screw on the lid and let the mixture age for a month, shaking it every so often. As you use the vanilla extract, top the jar off with more liquor, and replace any old vanilla beans every four months or so. You can even add any scraped vanilla bean pods to the jar. The longer the extract ages, the more potent it becomes.

# SUGAR 101

**Cane Sugar vs. Beet Sugar** We use Domino 100 percent pure cane sugar at our bakery. Beet sugar is often made from genetically modified (GMO) beets, and we avoid GMO foods wherever possible.

**Granulated Sugar** The most refined of all sugars, granulated sugar is the most commonly used sugar in baking. It adds sweetness and moisture to baked goods and helps them retain their structure. Granulated sugar also helps your pastries develop that beautiful and delicious caramel color and flavor.

**Confectioners' Sugar** Also called powdered sugar, confectioners' sugar is finely ground refined sugar that is mixed with cornstarch to prevent clumping. Confectioners' sugar is most commonly used for frostings, glazes and icings. If you find clumps in it (which you often will), sift it through a fine mesh sieve.

**Superfine Sugar** Also known as castor sugar, superfine sugar has the smallest crystals of all white granulated sugars and is often used in delicate or smooth desserts, such as puddings, mousses and meringues.

**Brown Sugar** A refined granulated sugar with cane molasses added back in. Light brown sugar contains less molasses (3½ percent) than dark brown sugar (6½ percent), which has a deeper and richer flavor. Brown sugar is very moist and can clump easily, so we recommend storing it in an airtight container after opening. To prevent brown sugars from hardening, add a piece of bread or a citrus peel (and replace it every 2-3 weeks) to the containers that they are stored in. The moisture from the bread or peel will keep the sugar soft.

Brown sugar adds moisture and helps your favorite baked goods, like cookies, spread and expand.

You can make your own light brown sugar: Mix together 1 pound granulated sugar and 3 ounces molasses in a food processor. Store in an airtight container.

**Raw Sugar** Raw sugar is an unrefined or partially refined sugar. It has a natural brown color and subtle to strong molasses flavors. There are different varieties of raw sugar (demerara, turbinado, muscovado), which vary in moisture content. Generally, we use crunchy turbinado sugar to top cookies, bars and pie crusts.

# A NOTE ON WEIGHING INGREDIENTS

As we sent out our recipes for testing, we heard from friends, colleagues and family that none of them used the weight measurements we had provided. So, we decided not to use them in our book unless we felt it was necessary for a recipe. Why? Our baking tends to be simple, and for many of

our recipes, all you will need is a whisk, a spatula, mixing bowls and measuring cups. You won't find finicky soufflés or yeasted breads in these pages.

However, if you are a person who prefers weights, we've created this handy conversion chart for you:

# Conversion Charts

## Weight Measurement Conversions

| U.S. | METRIC |
|------|--------|
| ¼ oz | 7 g |
| ½ oz | 15 g |
| 1 oz | 30 g |
| 2 oz | 60 g |
| 3 oz | 90 g |
| 4 oz | 113 g |
| 5 oz | 150 g |
| 6 oz | 170 g |
| 7 oz | 200 g |
| 8 oz (½ lb) | 225 g |
| 9 oz | 250 g |
| 10 oz | 300 g |
| 11 oz | 325 g |
| 12 oz | 350 g |
| 13 oz | 375 g |
| 14 oz | 400 g |
| 15 oz | 425 g |
| 16 oz (1 lb) | 450 g |
| 1½ lb | 750 g |
| 2 lb | 900 g |
| 2¼ lb | 1 kg |
| 3 lb | 1.4 kg |

## Oven Temperature Conversions

| GAS MARK | FAHRENHEIT | CELSIUS | GAS MARK |
|----------|-----------|---------|----------|
| ¼ | 225 | 107 | ¼ |
| ½ | 250 | 120 | ½ |
| 1 | 275 | 135 | 1 |
| 2 | 300 | 150 | 2 |
| 3 | 325 | 170 | 3 |
| 4 | 350 | 180 | 4 |
| 5 | 375 | 190 | 5 |
| 6 | 400 | 200 | 6 |
| 7 | 425 | 220 | 7 |
| 8 | 450 | 230 | 8 |
| 9 | 475 | 240 | 9 |

## Volume Measurement Conversions

| U.S. | METRIC | IMPERIAL |
|------|--------|----------|
| ¼ tsp | 1.2 ml | |
| ½ tsp | 2.5 ml | |
| 1 tsp | 5.0 ml | |
| 1 Tbsp (3 tsp) | 15 ml | ½ oz |
| ¼ cup (4 Tbsp) | 60 ml | 2 fl oz |
| ⅓ cup (5 Tbsp) | 80 ml | 2.5 fl oz |
| ½ cup (8 Tbsp) | 120 ml | 4 fl oz |
| ⅔ cup (10 Tbsp) | 160 ml | 5 fl oz |
| ¾ cup (12 Tbsp) | 180 ml | 6 fl oz |
| 1 cup (16 Tbsp) | 250 ml | 8 fl oz (½ pint) |
| 1¼ cups | 300 ml | 10 fl oz |
| 1½ cups | 350 ml | 12 fl oz |
| 2 cups | 475 ml | 16 fl oz (1 pint) |
| 2½ cups | 625 ml | 20 fl oz |
| 4 cups (1 quart) | 950 ml (1 liter) | 32 fl oz (2 pints) |

Note

While we aim to be as specific and as accurate as possible with our measurements, we must add the disclaimer that these are also approximations. Small but important factors, like climate, elevation and equipment, may impact procedures and final outcomes, but we hope that you can adjust as needed to make each recipe a huge success.

# SCONES
# & BISCUITS

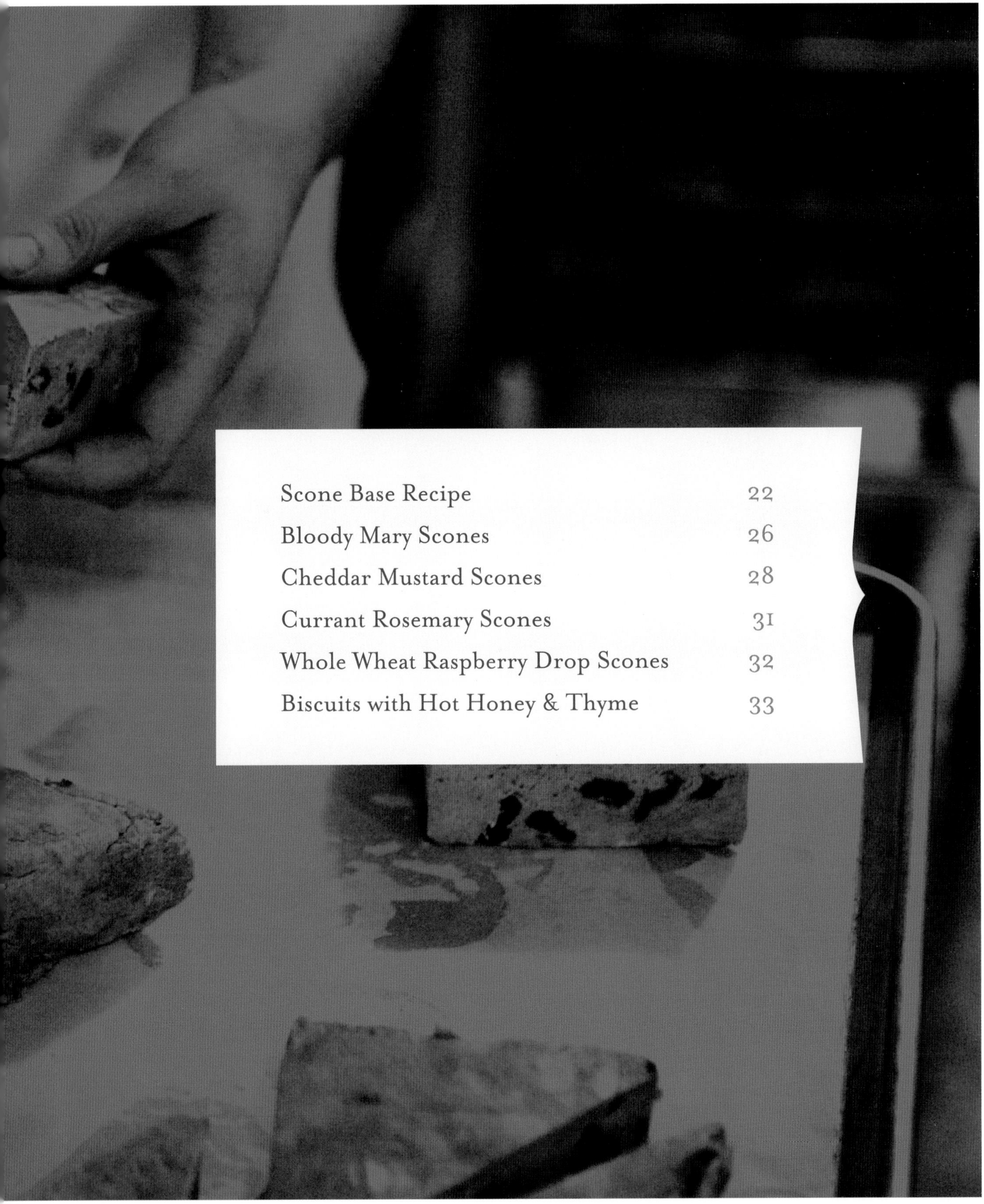

*Agatha* ❖ When you work endless hours in a bakery like Erin and I do, you end up eating whatever is immediately available, which means a lot of sweet stuff. A regular meal is often replaced by a misshapen cookie that's too odd looking to be sold but shouldn't go to waste, a few spoonfuls of gooey leftover batter, or a slice of cake that ends up being your breakfast, lunch and dinner. However, you can survive on an all-sugar regimen only for so long before you start feeling really, really weird. So after a few months in the trenches at Ovenly, Erin and I started to long for something savory. Our sweet tooth wanted salty, and cheesy scones and buttermilk biscuits were the fix we needed.

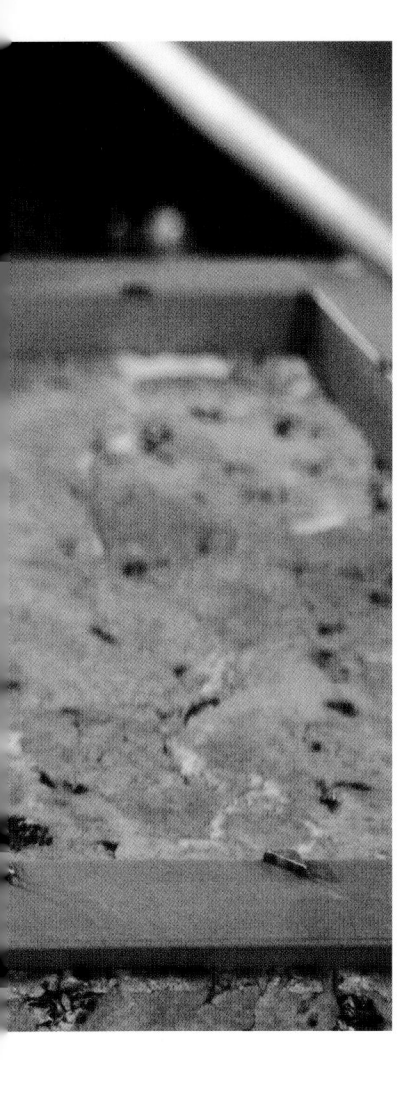

We know scones have a bad reputation for being dry and boring. We believed this ourselves until we started testing out our own. Our first flavor was a delicately sweet currant-rosemary scone. But our craving for salt drove us to experiment with other flavor combinations while fine-tuning our technique. Some of those flavors included black sesame–scallion, Parmesan-sage and blue cheese–pecan (which is still part of our repertoire).

Day after day, we created new flavors out of our tiny rented kitchen, then literally ran them to cafés and other clients. Those quick on-foot deliveries became somewhat of an Olympic sport (and our only exercise) until we bought Wedgie, our grumpy late-nineties Ford Explorer, months later. By the time we arrived with our deliveries, customers would be eagerly waiting to have their first pick of a hot, buttery scone. A woman once chased me down the street after discovering that the dozen or so scones we had just delivered were already sold out. She was hoping that I had one stashed in my purse, I guess. Sadly, I did not (but probably should have).

The demand for our scones began to increase at an intimidating speed. At the time, we were working out of the kitchen at Paulie Gee's—a rustic, dimly lit pizza joint in Greenpoint with a wood-burning oven that never completely cooled down. There we baked for a few predawn hours each day. Our work space consisted of two small inconveniently arranged prep areas. One was a little metal table in a tiny galley kitchen, where we did all our mixing. The other was a marble counter, perfect for rolling butter-based doughs.

It is important to know that crafting the perfect scone requires a few elemental factors: cold ingredients, a cool kitchen and lots of light. Unfortunately, the marble counter where we prepped the scones was positioned directly in front of the flaming, hot oven. And Paulie Gee's sexy mood lighting limited our visibility (though it's lovely). It was truly a baker's worst nightmare. The cards were stacked against us.

On a strangely hot day in late March 2011, with a huge number of orders to fill, I began our scone production next to my one true enemy (the pizza oven). It was a race against time, and I was already breaking a sweat. Though we had placed the ingredients in the freezer overnight, by the time I was cutting and shaping our scone dough, it was way too warm. With barely any light to actually see the flecks of butter melting into sad swirls throughout our dough, I soldiered on. However, as I fruitlessly attempted to divide and cut the dough into proper triangles, my hands became covered in a sticky, hot mess (insert expletives here). Things had gone from bad to worse. I desperately threw the melty scones into our freezer for ten minutes before baking them, hoping that this would somehow help them to retain their shape. I might have even done a little prayer dance in front of that pizza oven.

Sadly, my shamanism failed. Not only did the scones look like crumpled blobs, but they were also inedible. This was the first time we failed to deliver goods to our clients. As I dumped the worthless batch into the trash, I thought about the lines of excited customers at our clients' coffee shops. I thought about the woman who had chased me down the street with a twinkle of hope in her eye. And, although I am not a crier, I may have just cried a little that day.

The final straw came days later, when I accidentally melted sixteen pounds of frozen butter all over Paulie's floor (horrifying) while attempting to soften it in front of the pizza oven. I still have nightmares about cleaning up that oil spill. We love Paulie Gee and are ever grateful for his generosity during those memorable days, but by then we had grown up faster than we imagined. It was time to get a kitchen of our own.

For these scone and biscuit recipes, it is essential to start with really cold ingredients. Freeze butter before cutting it and mixing it into the dry ingredients. Quickly knead and fold the dough in order to keep it from warming up too much. You'll know that the dough is cold enough if you see solid bits of butter dispersed throughout. During baking, heat causes the water trapped in those cold butter flakes to turn to steam, which creates tiny air pockets. These are good! The result is flaky, layered perfection.

One last tip: Before you start baking, remember to keep away from blazing pizza ovens and make sure your conditions are optimal. And prepare yourself, as you may just be converted into a scone lover for life. We were.

# SCONE BASE RECIPE

*Yield: 8 scones*

*This scone base is the kind of recipe you write down once and never forget, one that you can magically whip up at a friend's house, for a brunch party or for breakfast in bed. Easily modifiable based on whether you're in a sweet or salty kind of mood, the flavor of these scones will depend on the quality of ingredients you use. These take minimal effort once you've got the technique down, and can be made in larger batches and frozen, so that they are ready to pop in the oven on any occasion. And remember, scones are like croissants: best eaten the same day they are baked (and even better when served warm).*

## SWEET SCONES

8 tablespoons (4 ounces) chilled, unsalted butter

3 cups all-purpose flour

¼ cup + 1 tablespoon sugar

1½ tablespoons baking powder

¾ teaspoon salt

1 cup additions, such as fruit, cheese or herbs (if using)

1½ cups chilled heavy cream + more for brushing

Turbinado sugar, for garnish

## SAVORY SCONES

*Substitute:* Use only 1 tablespoon sugar and increase salt to 1¼ teaspoons

Top with coarse sea salt and freshly cracked black pepper

1. Preheat the oven to 425°F.

2. Cut the butter into ¼- to ½-inch cubes and freeze for 10 minutes before using. Whisk together the flour, sugar, baking powder and salt in a large bowl.

3. Using a pastry cutter or your fingertips, quickly cut or blend the cold butter into the dry mixture until it resembles coarse meal. The butter pieces should be mostly about the size of small pebbles, but some larger pieces are okay. See Scone Process on pages 24–25.

4. Using a large fork or a wooden spoon, mix your desired additions into the flour-butter mixture.

5. Stir the cream into the flour-butter mixture with a large wooden spoon or a fork until the dough begins to come together. The flour should not be fully incorporated at this point, and do not overmix.

6. Transfer the dough and any loose floury bits to a floured countertop or pastry board/mat.

7. Quickly knead the dough until it comes fully together, and then flatten it with the palms of your hands into a ¾-inch-thick mound (the shape does not matter at this point). Fold the dough in half, give it a quarter turn and then flatten it again. Repeat this process 3 more times.

8. Flour your surface once more, and then shape the dough into a ¾-inch-thick round that is 6 inches in diameter. Use a bench scraper or a knife to cut the dough into 4 equal triangles. Then cut those in half to make 8 even triangles. Place the triangles on an ungreased rimmed sheet pan.

9. At this point, we recommend placing the rimmed sheet pan in the freezer for 10 minutes. This will help the scones firm up and retain their shape during baking. If baking right away, brush with cream and top with turbinado sugar or salt and pepper to finish; or if freezing, brush with cream and top with turbinado sugar or salt and pepper just before baking.

10. Bake for 18 to 20 minutes, or until the tops are golden brown and a toothpick inserted in the center of the scones comes out clean. Cool the scones on a wire rack. Serve warm with butter, jam or honey.

### Sweet Variations

· Apricot–fresh thyme—Add 1 cup chopped dried or fresh apricots and 2 teaspoons chopped fresh thyme

· Dried plum–candied ginger— Add ¾ cup of chopped dried plums and ¼ cup (packed) finely chopped candied ginger

· Cinnamon–milk chocolate—Add 3 tablespoons ground cinnamon and 1 cup chopped milk chocolate

· Cherry–vanilla—Add 1 cup dried sour cherries and mix 1 tablespoon vanilla extract into the heavy cream

### Savory Variations

· Blue cheese–pecan—Add ¾ cup crumbled blue cheese and ⅓ cup chopped pecans

· Gouda–pear—Add ¾ cup shredded Gouda and ⅓ cup chopped dried pears

· Parmesan–sage—Add 1 cup grated Parmesan and 2 tablespoons chopped fresh sage

· Black sesame–scallion—Add 1 cup (packed) sliced scallions and ¼ cup black sesame seeds, and mix 2 tablespoons sesame oil into the heavy cream

13

## SCONE PROCESS

01 Add the cubed butter to the flour mixture.

02 Cut the butter into the flour mixture, gently removing any butter pieces that get caught in the pastry cutter as you go and reincorporating them into the batter.

03 The mixture should resemble coarse meal, with varied pebble-size pieces of butter throughout.

04 After mixing in your additions, pour cream over the flour-butter mixture.

05 Stir in the cream until a dough begins to form. There should still be floury bits in the dough.

06 Gather the dough into a large mound.

07 Transfer the ball of dough, along with any loose flour bits, to a floured surface and knead until it just comes together. Flatten to about ¾-inch thick.

08 Fold the dough in half and give it a quarter turn.

09 Flatten the dough with the palms of your hands.

10 Re-flour your work surface, as needed.

11 Flatten, fold and turn the dough 3 more times.

12 Pat and shape the dough lightly into an even ¾-inch-thick round that is 6 inches in diameter.

13 Use a bench scraper or a knife to cut the dough into 4 equal triangles. Then cut those in half to make 8 even triangles.

# BLOODY MARY SCONES

*Yield: 8 scones*

*This recipe was conceived on a busy day in the kitchen when we had to miss out on brunch but craved a cold, spicy Bloody Mary. You can prepare it as is, or make it boozy by mixing some vodka or tequila into the cream. Speared with an olive and a cornichon, this is a hearty breakfast beverage disguised as a scone.*

8 tablespoons (4 ounces) chilled, unsalted butter

3 cups all-purpose flour

1 tablespoon sugar

1½ tablespoons baking powder

1 teaspoon salt

1 teaspoon paprika

¾ teaspoon ground fennel seed

½ teaspoon ground black pepper

¼ teaspoon cayenne pepper

¼ teaspoon garlic salt

½ cup oil-packed sun-dried tomatoes

2 small plum tomatoes, chopped into small pieces, seeded and liquid removed

2 tablespoons Worcestershire sauce

2 tablespoons + ½ tablespoon prepared horseradish

2 tablespoons Tabasco sauce

1¼ cups + 2 tablespoons chilled heavy cream + more for brushing

Red pepper flakes and celery salt, for garnish

**1.** Preheat the oven to 425°F.

**2.** Cut the butter into ¼- to ½-inch cubes and freeze for 10 minutes before using. Whisk together the flour, sugar, baking powder, salt, spices and garlic salt in a large bowl. Set aside.

**3.** In a food processor fitted with a blade attachment, puree the sun-dried tomatoes. It will yield about ¼ cup of puree.

**4.** Using a pastry cutter or your fingertips, quickly cut or blend the cold butter into the dry mixture until it resembles coarse meal. The butter pieces should be mostly about the size of small pebbles, but some larger pieces are okay.

**5.** Using a spoon or your hands, mix the chopped tomatoes into the flour-butter mixture.

**6.** Whisk the sun-dried tomato puree, Worcestershire, 2 tablespoons of the horseradish and the Tabasco into 1¼ cups of the chilled cream. Stir the cream mixture into the flour-butter mixture with a large wooden spoon or a fork until dough begins to come together. The flour-butter mixture should not be fully incorporated at this point, and do not overmix.

**7.** Transfer the dough and any loose floury bits to a floured countertop or pastry board/mat.

**8.** Quickly knead the dough until it comes fully together, and then flatten it with the palms of your hands into a ¾-inch-thick mound (the shape does not matter at this point). Fold the dough in half, give it a quarter turn and then flatten it again. Repeat this process 3 more times.

**9.** Flour your surface once more, and then shape the dough into a ¾-inch-thick round that is 6 inches in diameter. Use a bench scraper or a knife to cut the dough into 4 equal triangles. Then cut those in half to make 8 even triangles. Place the triangles on an ungreased rimmed sheet pan.

**10.** Mix the remaining cup cream with the remaining 2 tablespoons horseradish. Use a pastry brush to brush each triangle with the cream, and then top each with a few red pepper flakes and a generous sprinkling of celery salt.

8 toothpicks

8 cornichons (small pickles)

8 olives

*Go crazy with the garnish!
Any Bloody Mary-esque
condiments, such as
caperberries, pearled onions
or celery, work with these.*

**11.** At this point, we recommend placing the rimmed sheet pan in the freezer for 10 minutes. This will help the scones firm up and retain their shape during baking. If baking right away, brush with cream and top with red pepper flakes and celery salt to finish; or if freezing, brush with cream and top with garnish just before baking.

**12.** Bake for 18 to 20 minutes, or until the tops are golden brown and a toothpick inserted in the center of the scones comes out clean.

**13.** While the scones are baking, prepare the garnish for the scones. Skewer 8 toothpicks with 1 cornichon and 1 olive (or other garnishes of choice).

**14.** Cool the scones on a wire rack. Once cooled, stick a garnished toothpick in the top of each scone and serve.

## Get Creative

### Other Scone Ideas

· After brushing with cream, top your scones with turbinado sugar or coarse-grained sea salt, which adds a great crunch.

· If using fresh fruit or another "wet" ingredient, use a little less cream.

· Substitute half of the all-purpose flour with whole wheat flour for a heartier scone and a nutty flavor.

· Experiment with additions of various fresh and dried herbs and spices and citrus zest.

# CHEDDAR MUSTARD SCONES

*Yield: 8 scones*

*Living in New York City, we are spoiled with loads of handcrafted foods that are often too tempting to resist. So when we received a sample jar of gorgeous, thick whole-grain mustard that resembled oozy caviar, we got to experimenting with it. The end result was this beauty—light and cheesy, with tangy, crunchy pops of flavor throughout. We love to relish in the brief expressions of shock when people find out the secret ingredient is mustard; you'd never guess it.*

3 cups all-purpose flour

1½ tablespoons baking powder

1 tablespoon sugar

1¼ teaspoons salt

½ teaspoon mustard powder

8 tablespoons (4 ounces) unsalted butter, chilled and cut into ¼- to ½-inch cubes

1 cup (4 ounces) shredded sharp white cheddar

3 tablespoons whole-grain mustard (we recommend Tin or Maille)

1½ cups chilled heavy cream + more for brushing

Coarse sea salt and freshly cracked black pepper, for garnish

**1.** Preheat the oven to 425°F.

**2.** In a large bowl, whisk together the flour, baking powder, sugar, salt and mustard powder.

**3.** Using a pastry cutter or your fingertips, quickly cut or blend the cold butter into the dry mixture until it resembles coarse meal. The butter pieces should be mostly about the size of small pebbles, but some larger pieces are okay.

**4.** Using a large fork or a wooden spoon, mix the white cheddar into the flour-butter mixture.

**5.** Stir the wet whole-grain mustard into the cream until well combined. Then stir the cream mixture into the flour-butter mixture with a large wooden spoon or a fork until the dough begins to come together. The flour-butter mixture should not be fully incorporated at this point, and do not overmix.

**6.** Transfer the dough and any loose floury bits to a floured countertop or pastry board/mat.

**7.** Quickly knead the dough until it comes fully together, and then flatten it with the palms of your hands into a ¾-inch-thick mound that is 6 inches in diameter (the shape does not matter at this point). Fold the dough in half, give it a quarter turn and then flatten it again. Repeat this process 3 more times.

**8.** Flour your surface once more, and then shape the dough into a ¾-inch-thick round that is 6 inches in diameter. Use a bench scraper or a knife to cut the dough into 4 equal triangles. Then cut those in half to make 8 even triangles. Place the triangles on an ungreased rimmed sheet pan.

**9.** At this point, we recommend placing the rimmed sheet pan in the freezer for 10 minutes. This will help the scones firm up and retain their shape during baking. If baking right away, brush with cream and top with salt and pepper to finish; or if freezing, brush with cream and top with salt and pepper just before baking.

**10.** Bake for 18 to 20 minutes, or until the tops are golden brown and a toothpick inserted in the center of the scones comes out clean. Cool the scones on a wire rack. Serve warm with butter, jam or our favorite, Mike's Hot Honey.

# CURRANT ROSEMARY SCONES

*Yield: 8 scones*

*This was the first scone flavor we ever created at Ovenly, and it continues to be our most popular. My failed hunt to find fresh currants, which I've loved since I was a kid, inspired us to add dried currants to our dough. The fresh rosemary adds an herby aroma reminiscent of a summer garden. While they can easily be made in small batches, our bakers now make these in batches of many thousands at a time. Mounds of scone dough are rolled into sheet pans and then cut by hand. A lot of care (and muscle!) goes into making these scones.*

8 tablespoons (4 ounces) chilled, unsalted butter

3 cups all-purpose flour

¼ cup + 1 tablespoon sugar

1½ tablespoons baking powder

¾ teaspoon salt

1 cup dried currants

2 tablespoons finely chopped fresh rosemary

1½ cups chilled heavy cream + more for brushing

2 to 3 tablespoons turbinado sugar, for garnish

**1.** Preheat the oven to 425°F.

**2.** Cut the butter into ¼- to ½-inch cubes and freeze for 10 minutes before using. Whisk together the flour, sugar, baking powder and salt in a large bowl.

**3.** Using a pastry cutter or your fingertips, quickly cut or blend the cold butter into the dry mixture until it resembles coarse meal. The butter pieces should be mostly about the size of small pebbles, but some larger pieces are okay.

**4.** Using a large fork or a wooden spoon, mix the currants and rosemary into the flour-butter mixture.

**5.** Stir the cream into the flour-butter mixture with a large wooden spoon or a fork until the dough begins to come together. The flour should not be fully incorporated at this point, and do not overmix.

**6.** Transfer the dough and any loose floury bits to a floured countertop or pastry board/mat.

**7.** Quickly knead the dough until it comes fully together, and then flatten it with the palms of your hands into a ¾-inch-thick mound (the shape does not matter at this point). Fold the dough in half, give it a quarter turn and then flatten it again. Repeat this process 3 more times.

**8.** Flour your surface once more, and then shape the dough into a ¾-inch-thick round that is 6 inches in diameter. Use a bench scraper or a knife to cut the dough into 4 equal triangles. Then cut those in half to make 8 even triangles. Place the triangles on an ungreased rimmed sheet pan.

**9.** At this point, we recommend placing the rimmed sheet pan in the freezer for 10 minutes. This will help the scones firm up and retain their shape during baking. If baking right away, brush with cream and top with turbinado sugar to finish; or if freezing, brush with cream and top with turbinado sugar just before baking.

**10.** Bake for 18 to 20 minutes, or until the tops are golden brown and a toothpick inserted in the center of the scones comes out clean. Cool the scones on a wire rack. Serve warm with butter, jam or honey.

# WHOLE WHEAT RASPBERRY DROP SCONES

*Yield: 8 scones*

*Certain baking projects can demand a serious time commitment. Luckily, this is not one of them! You can throw these suckers together in minutes, and there is no precision needed in shaping them—just use a large spoon or cookie scoop and drop the dough in small mounds onto your rimmed sheet pan. The end result will be scones that appear rustic yet are refined in texture and flavor.*

Nonstick cooking spray

8 tablespoons (4 ounces) chilled, unsalted butter

1¼ cups whole-wheat pastry flour

¾ cup all-purpose flour

2 tablespoons sugar

1 tablespoon baking powder

1 teaspoon (packed) lemon zest

½ teaspoon salt

¾ cup raspberries, preferably frozen

¼ cup maple syrup (the darker the better; we use Grade B)

½ cup heavy cream

1 large egg, lightly beaten

Turbinado sugar or maple sugar, for garnish

**1.** Preheat the oven to 400°F. Spray a rimmed sheet pan with nonstick cooking spray or line it with parchment paper.

**2.** Cut the butter into ¼- to ½-inch cubes and freeze for 10 minutes before using. In a large bowl, whisk together the flours, sugar, baking powder, lemon zest and salt. In a small bowl, reserve ¼ cup of the flour mixture and set aside.

**3.** Using a pastry cutter or your fingertips, quickly cut or blend the cold butter into the dry mixture until it resembles coarse meal. The butter pieces should be mostly about the size of small pebbles, but some larger pieces are okay.

**4.** Add the raspberries to the reserved flour mixture. Stir carefully, coating the fruit evenly. Gently mix them into the flour-butter mixture.

**5.** Whisk the maple syrup into the cream to combine.

**6.** Make a well in the flour-butter mixture, and add the cream–maple syrup mixture and the egg. Stir with a large wooden spoon or fork, and mix evenly until the dough just comes together. Ensure that the floury bits are fully incorporated, but do not overmix.

**7.** Using a large spoon or a scoop, drop 8 equally sized mounds of dough onto the prepared rimmed sheet pan.

**8.** At this point, we recommend placing the rimmed sheet pan in the freezer for 10 minutes. This will help the scones from spreading too much during baking. Top each ball of dough with a sprinkle of turbinado or maple sugar before baking.

**9.** Bake for 16 to 18 minutes, or until the tops are golden brown and a toothpick inserted in the center of the scones comes out clean. Cool the scones on a wire rack.

# BISCUITS WITH HOT HONEY & THYME

*Yield: 8 biscuits*

*My love for fried chicken, pimento cheese sandwiches and brisket is trumped by one thing only: biscuits. Everyone has an opinion about the method for making a proper biscuit. We're of the opinion that if it tastes like and resembles a buttery, flaky mound of heaven, it is a damn good biscuit, especially when you add a healthy dose of Mike's Hot Honey and fresh thyme.*

---

Softened butter or nonstick cooking spray, for greasing the rimmed sheet pan

18 tablespoons (9 ounces) unsalted butter + 3 tablespoons butter, for melting

5 cups all-purpose flour

2 tablespoons sugar

2 tablespoons baking powder

1 tablespoon salt

1 tablespoon + 1 teaspoon chopped fresh thyme

6 tablespoons Mike's Hot Honey + more for drizzling

2 cups cold buttermilk

**1.** Preheat the oven to 400°F. Grease a rimmed sheet pan with softened butter or nonstick cooking spray.

**2.** Cut 18 tablespoons of the butter into ½-inch cubes. Place the butter cubes in a small bowl and freeze for at least 10 minutes.

**3.** In a large bowl, whisk together the flour, sugar, baking powder, salt and 1 tablespoon of the thyme. Add the frozen butter cubes to the flour mixture and toss to coat. Working quickly, use your hands or a pastry cutter to cut the butter into the flour mixture until it resembles coarse meal. The butter pieces should be mostly about the size of small pebbles, but some larger pieces are okay.

**4.** Whisk 3 tablespoons of the honey into 1¾ cups cold buttermilk (reserve the ¼ cup remaining buttermilk for later if needed). Using a spatula or wooden spoon, incorporate the honey-buttermilk mixture into the flour-butter mixture. Ensure the flour at the bottom of the bowl has been incorporated into the dough. If the dough seems too dry, add the reserved ¼ cup buttermilk, as needed, until the loose flour bits have been incorporated into the dough. Turn the dough onto a floured surface.

**5.** Pat the dough into a rectangle about a ½ inch thick that is approximately 12 x 6-inches. Fold the dough into thirds (like you would a letter), and gently pat down again into a uniform rectangle of ¾-inch thickness. Cut into 8 squares (two rows of 4 squares).

**6.** Place the biscuits onto the prepared sheet pan, and bake for 18 minutes. The biscuits will be light golden. Remove from the oven.

**7.** While the biscuits bake, melt the remaining 3 tablespoons butter in a small saucepan. Remove from heat, and mix in the other 3 tablespoons honey and the remaining 1 teaspoon thyme. Remove the biscuits from the oven, and reduce the oven temperature to 350°F. Brush the hot biscuits with the melted butter mixture, and then return to the oven. Bake them for 10 minutes more, or until deep golden brown.

**8.** Drizzle the biscuits with additional honey. Serve warm.

# QUICK BREADS
# & COFFEE CAKES

*Erin* ❖ Heather Millstone, the owner of Veronica People's Club (VPC) and also our first client, had given us one directive: "Bake whatever you want, but there has to be savory, gluten-free stuff on the menu." At the time, Agatha and I had been talking for a year about what kind of food company, exactly, we would start together, so when Heather gave us the opportunity to create the morning pastries and baked goods for her café, we hastily said yes. When she asked us for something wheat free, we shrugged and thought, *How hard could that be?* Turns out, the answer is, *Pretty freaking hard.*

One morning soon after, I found myself tiptoeing around my apartment at 4:00 a.m., attempting to be as quiet as possible (my roommates had become rightfully irritated with my daily early morning baking sessions) while I followed a questionable potato flour–based walnut bread recipe that I had uncovered somewhere in the depths of the food blogosphere. I winced at the sound of ripping plastic as I tore open bags of arrowroot starch and xanthan gum, and at the clank of glass as I searched for mace in my spice cabinet.

The recipe called for the rubbery batter to be blended, oddly, in the food processor, where it now whirred noisily and spiritlessly. I pulled the bowl from the machine and tasted the voluminous dough. It was both sour and bitter, and something in the batter—maybe the buttermilk powder or the guar gum or the gluten-free beer— spread an unpleasant, numbing tingle over my tongue and down into my throat.

But, as usual, I was running late and was out of ideas. I took a chance and put the loaf pan into the oven, hoping the bread would miraculously taste delicious once baked. Later that day, the verdict came via a text from Agatha:

"Whatever that nut thing is at Veronica's, it tastes scary."

My heart dropped into my gut.

As evidenced by the near paralysis of my tongue, our strategy of Google-searching the words "taste good gluten-free salt easy fast" for recipes clearly wasn't working. Our VPC experiments came at a time when Ovenly consisted of me and Agatha baking in our tiny apartments and hand-delivering our freshly baked treats to locations all over New York City by any means necessary. I'm talking subways, cabs, speed walking, bikes, you name it. We were already busy with the logistics of just running the business, and we were tired of struggling to resolve this savory dilemma.

That fateful gummy batter was the last straw in this trial-and-error adventure. We had had it up to here with exotic flours and mystery thickeners, and resolved to use only ingredients that we knew and trusted. Together, we made a pact to invent recipes—gluten-free or not—that resulted in treats we actually *wanted* to eat, regardless of our clients' imperatives. This meant more cookies and cakes made with all-natural ingredients, more delectable morning buns, and heartier muffins made with dried fruits and natural oils. We ceremoniously tore the walnut bread printout to shreds. The demons had been exorcised.

For inspiration, Agatha and I started by thinking about our favorite childhood cravings. Both of us grew up in the 1980s, when most so-called "homemade" pastries we ate actually came from a mix or were reheated from frozen in oven-ready aluminum packaging. Some of that stuff was probably made mostly from additives and food coloring, but, man, was it delicious. Who doesn't remember devouring the crumb topping off of Entenmann's Devil's Food Crumb Donuts? Or unrolling a Sara Lee Cinnamon Roll from end to center and eating it in one long strip? Or picking the tiny dehydrated blueberries out of each Duncan Hines just-add-water muffin? The question for us now was, How could we make those memories come alive for Ovenly's sweets and savories? Quick breads and coffee cakes fit into our quest to make simple, delicious and edible treats—a core facet of our business today.

We started testing like crazy. And, as we grew more experienced, we stopped reinventing the wheel with each new try. Instead, we came up with bases that could be easily altered and augmented, and we got creative with all the little mounds of unused ingredients we had on hand from our R & D. Random almond shards + white chocolate chips from that popover-type thing that didn't turn out = almond–white chocolate coffee cake. Lemon zest + a bunch of half-used bags of frozen fruit = berry-citrus bread. Voilà!

This chapter illustrates how to make top-notch versions of our favorite quick breads and coffee cakes. Many of our greatest triumphs occurred once we stopped trying so hard to fit into a particular mold, and started to simply bake with our hearts (and our guts!). This is an important lesson that we are happy to share with our readers, and we encourage you to throw in those leftover bits and pieces to invent something all your own.

# QUICK BREAD BASE RECIPE

*Yield: one 9 x 5-inch loaf*

*As with our coffee cake, we experimented for weeks to create a perfect quick bread base. With the mix of agave and sugars, this recipe will never be too sweet. Dense and moist, it provides a great foundation for fruits, citrus, chocolate chunks and spice.*

Softened unsalted butter, canola oil or nonstick cooking spray, for greasing the loaf pan

½ cup (4 ounces) unsalted butter

1 cup buttermilk

½ cup sugar

¼ cup (packed) light brown sugar

¼ cup liquid sugar, such as agave nectar, maple syrup* or honey

2 large eggs, at room temperature

2 cups + ¼ cup flour (try using a mix of all-purpose, whole-wheat or oat)

1 teaspoon baking soda

1 teaspoon baking powder

1 teaspoon salt

Zest of 1 lemon, orange or lime (optional)

### ADDITIONS

1 cup berries (fresh or frozen)

1 cup semisweet chocolate chips

½ cup toasted, chopped nuts

Chopped fresh herbs, to taste OR 1 to 2 teaspoons of your favorite dried spice (added into the flour-baking soda mix)

*\*The darker the better; we prefer Grade B*

**1.** Preheat the oven to 350°F. Grease a 9 x 5-inch loaf pan with softened butter, canola oil or nonstick cooking spray.

**2.** In a small saucepan over low heat (or in a small, microwave-safe bowl in a microwave oven), melt the butter and set aside to cool.

**3.** In a large bowl, whisk together buttermilk, all sugars, eggs and the melted butter until well blended.

**4.** In a separate large bowl, whisk together 2 cups of the flour, baking soda, baking powder, salt and zest (if using).

**5.** In a small bowl, mix together the remaining ¼ cup flour and the additions you desire.

**6.** Using a spatula or a wooden spoon, mix the dry ingredients into the wet ingredients until almost combined. Fold in any additions until just incorporated.

**7.** Pour the batter into the prepared loaf pan and bake for 50 to 55 minutes, or until a toothpick inserted in the center of the loaf comes out clean.

**8.** Let the loaf cool completely before slicing.

# CITRUS BERRY QUICK BREAD

*Yield: one 9 x 5-inch loaf*

*In New York, berry season means five-gallon buckets of freshly picked fruit delivered to our bakery. We add them to everything, including our quick breads.*

Softened unsalted butter, canola oil or nonstick cooking spray, for greasing the loaf pan

½ cup (4 ounces) unsalted butter

1 cup buttermilk

½ cup sugar

½ cup (packed) light brown sugar

¼ cup agave nectar

2 large eggs, at room temperature

1¼ cups + 1 tablespoon all-purpose flour

1 cup whole-wheat pastry flour

1 teaspoon baking soda

1 teaspoon baking powder

1 teaspoon salt

Zest of 1 lemon

½ cup blackberries (fresh or frozen)

½ cup raspberries (fresh or frozen)

1. Preheat the oven to 350°F. Grease a 9 x 5-inch loaf pan with softened butter, canola oil or nonstick cooking spray.

2. In a small saucepan over low heat (or in a small, microwave-safe bowl in a microwave oven), melt the butter and set aside to cool.

3. In a large bowl, whisk together the buttermilk, all sugars, agave, eggs and melted butter until well blended.

4. In a separate large bowl, whisk together 1¼ cups of the all-purpose flour, whole-wheat pastry flour, baking soda, baking powder, salt and lemon zest.

5. In a small bowl, mix together the remaining 1 tablespoon all-purpose flour and the fruit to coat.

6. Using a spatula or a wooden spoon, mix the dry ingredients into the wet ingredients until almost combined. Gently fold in the fruit until just coated.

7. Pour the batter into the prepared loaf pan and bake for 50 to 55 minutes, or until a toothpick inserted in the center of the loaf comes out clean.

8. Let the loaf cool completely before slicing.

# STRAWBERRY BASIL LOAF

*Yield: one 9 x 5-inch loaf*

Softened unsalted butter, canola oil or nonstick cooking spray, for greasing the loaf pan

½ cup (4 ounces) unsalted butter

1 cup buttermilk

½ cup sugar

¼ cup (packed) light brown sugar

¼ cup maple syrup (the darker the better; we use Grade B)

2 large eggs, at room temperature

2¼ cups + 2 tablespoons all-purpose flour

1 teaspoon baking soda

1 teaspoon baking powder

1 teaspoon salt

Zest of 1 lemon

1¼ cups chopped fresh strawberries

1 tablespoon chopped fresh basil

**1.** Preheat the oven to 350°F. Liberally grease a 9 x 5-inch loaf pan with softened butter, canola oil or nonstick cooking spray.

**2.** In a small saucepan over low heat (or in a small, microwave-safe bowl in a microwave oven), melt the butter and set aside to cool.

**3.** In a large bowl, whisk together the buttermilk, all sugars, maple syrup, eggs and melted butter until well blended.

**4.** In a separate large bowl, whisk together 2¼ cups of the flour, baking soda, baking powder, salt and lemon zest.

**5.** In a small bowl, mix together the remaining 2 tablespoons flour and the strawberries to coat.

**6.** Using a spatula or a wooden spoon, mix the dry ingredients into the wet ingredients until almost combined. Gently fold in the strawberries and the basil until just coated.

**7.** Pour the batter into the prepared loaf pan and bake for 45 minutes, or until a toothpick inserted in the center of the loaf comes out clean.

**8.** Let the loaf cool completely before slicing.

## Get Creative

### Flavor Combinations with a Twist

· Raspberry-Cardamom—1 cup fresh or frozen raspberries, 1½ teaspoons ground cardamom

· Blueberry-Lime—1 cup fresh or frozen blueberries, zest of 1 lime

· Fresh Apricot-Vanilla Bean—1 cup chopped fresh apricots, seeds from 1 vanilla bean

· Milk Chocolate-Pine Nut—1 cup chopped milk chocolate, ½ cup toasted pine nuts, 2 teaspoons ground cinnamon

 *Dip your offset spatula in hot water as you spread the batter in the pan for smooth and even layers.*

# COFFEE CAKE BASE RECIPE

*Yield: one 13 x 9-inch cake, cut into 12 pieces*

*This basic recipe is just the right combination of dense and fluffy and is a keystone for any flavor combination you could possibly think of. Play with the filling measurements as you go along to find the perfect balance of flavors. For example, use 1 cup of peanut butter and ½ cup of your favorite jam as the filling, or use ¾ cup of chocolate chips with ½ cup of toasted pecans and ½ cup of dark brown sugar.*

Softened unsalted butter and all-purpose flour, for preparing the baking pan

1 cup (16 tablespoons, 8 ounces) unsalted butter

3¾ cups all-purpose flour

2 cups sugar

1 tablespoon baking powder

1½ teaspoons salt

¼ teaspoon baking soda

1 cup buttermilk

4 large eggs, at room temperature

¼ cup sour cream (preferably full-fat)

2 teaspoons vanilla extract

Coffee Cake Streusel (see recipe on page 46)

**1.** Preheat the oven to 350°F. Grease a 13 x 9-inch baking pan with softened butter and dust the pan with flour.

**2.** In a small saucepan over low heat (or in a small, microwave-safe bowl in a microwave oven), melt the butter and set aside to cool.

**3.** In a large bowl, whisk together the flour, sugar, baking powder, salt and baking soda.

**4.** In a separate large bowl, whisk together the buttermilk, eggs, sour cream, vanilla extract and melted butter until very smooth.

**5.** Using a spatula or a wooden spoon, mix the dry ingredients into the wet ingredients until combined.

**6.** Layer half of the batter in the prepared baking pan, smoothing it out to the edges and leveling the top. This batter is thick, so evenly spoon or scoop it in tablespoon-size mounds into the pan before spreading. Use the back of a spoon or an offset spatula (this works best) to smooth it in the pan.

**7.** Spread the desired filling evenly over the batter, and then layer the remaining batter over the filling, using the same method of spooning or scooping. Smooth out the top of the batter, ensuring it is even and reaches the edges of the pan.

**8.** Sprinkle the top with streusel, and then bake for 50 to 55 minutes, or until a toothpick inserted in the center of the cake comes out clean.

## Get Creative

### Other Scrumptious Fillings

- ½ cup cashew butter, ½ cup light brown sugar, ½ teaspoon cayenne pepper

- 1 cup chopped milk chocolate, 1 teaspoon ground cinnamon

- ½ cup pistachio meal, 2 tablespoons honey (honey tends to soak into the cake, so be light-handed with it), zest of 1 orange

- ¾ cup chopped toasted walnuts, ½ cup dark brown sugar, ½ cup dried currants

# BANANA NUTELLA COFFEE CAKE

*Yield: one 13 x 9-inch cake, cut into 12 pieces*

*We love the classic combination of sweet bananas and creamy Nutella for coffee cake filling. Nutella retains its consistency when baked inside a dough or batter, so it looks beautiful when the cake is sliced.*

Softened unsalted butter and all-purpose flour, for preparing the baking pan

### CAKE

1 cup (16 tablespoons, 8 ounces) unsalted butter

3¾ cups all-purpose flour

2 cups sugar

1 tablespoon baking powder

1½ teaspoons salt

¼ teaspoon baking soda

1 cup buttermilk

4 large eggs, at room temperature

¼ cup sour cream (preferably full-fat)

2 teaspoons vanilla extract

### FILLING

2 small ripe bananas, peeled and thinly sliced

½ cup Nutella, or another hazelnut-chocolate spread

¼ cup (packed) light brown sugar

### TOPPING

Coffee Cake Streusel (see recipe on page 46)

**1.** Preheat the oven to 350°F. Grease a 13 x 9-inch baking pan with softened butter and dust the pan with flour.

**2.** In a small saucepan over low heat (or in a small, microwave-safe bowl in a microwave oven), melt the butter and set aside to cool.

**3.** In a large bowl, whisk together the flour, sugar, baking powder, salt and baking soda.

**4.** In a separate large bowl, whisk together the buttermilk, eggs, sour cream, vanilla extract and melted butter until very smooth.

**5.** Using a spatula or a wooden spoon, mix the dry ingredients into the wet ingredients until combined.

**6.** Layer half of the batter in the prepared baking pan, smoothing it out to the edges and leveling the top. This batter is thick, so evenly spoon or scoop it in tablespoon-size mounds into the pan before spreading. Use the back of a spoon or an offset spatula (this works best) to smooth it in the pan.

**7.** Spread the banana slices evenly over the batter, overlapping the slices. Drizzle the Nutella over the bananas (if it's too thick, melt it in a small saucepan over very low heat, or in a small, microwave-safe bowl in a microwave oven for 15 seconds). Sprinkle with the light brown sugar.

**8.** Layer the remaining batter over the filling using the same method of spooning or scooping. Smooth out the top of the batter, ensuring it is even and reaches the edges of the pan.

**9.** Sprinkle the top with streusel, and then bake for 50 to 55 minutes, or until a toothpick inserted in the center of the cake comes out clean.

# POPPY SEED, PRUNE & LEMON COFFEE CAKE

*Yield: one 13 x 9-inch cake, cut into 12 pieces*

*Playing off Eastern European flavors, this coffee cake combines some of our favorite ingredients.*

Softened unsalted butter and all-purpose flour, for preparing the baking pan

### CAKE

1 cup (16 tablespoons, 8 ounces) unsalted butter

3¾ cups all-purpose flour

2 cups sugar

1 tablespoon baking powder

1½ teaspoons salt

¼ teaspoon baking soda

1 cup buttermilk

4 large eggs, at room temperature

¼ cup sour cream (preferably full-fat)

2 teaspoons vanilla extract

### FILLING

½ cup (about 16) chopped prunes

½ cup (packed) dark brown sugar

¼ cup poppy seeds

Zest of 1 lemon

### TOPPING

Coffee Cake Streusel (see recipe on page 46)

**1.** Preheat the oven to 350°F. Grease a 13 x 9-inch baking pan with softened butter and dust the pan with flour.

**2.** In a small saucepan over low heat (or in a small, microwave-safe bowl in a microwave oven), melt the butter and set aside to cool.

**3.** In a large bowl, whisk together the flour, sugar, baking powder, salt and baking soda.

**4.** In a separate large bowl, whisk together the buttermilk, eggs, sour cream, vanilla extract and melted butter until very smooth.

**5.** Using a spatula or a wooden spoon, mix the dry ingredients into the wet ingredients until combined.

**6.** Layer half of the batter in the prepared baking pan, smoothing it out to the edges and leveling the top. This batter is thick, so evenly spoon or scoop it in tablespoon-size mounds into the pan before spreading. Use the back of a spoon or an offset spatula (this works best) to smooth it in the pan.

**7.** Spread the prunes evenly over the batter. Sprinkle with the dark brown sugar and then the poppy seeds. Top the filling with the lemon zest.

**8.** Layer the remaining batter over the filling using the same method of spooning or scooping. Smooth out the top of the batter, ensuring it is even and reaches the edges of the pan.

**9.** Sprinkle the top with streusel, and then bake for 50 to 55 minutes, or until a toothpick inserted in the center of the cake comes out clean.

# COFFEE CAKE STREUSEL

*Yield: streusel for 1 coffee cake*

*We developed this streusel specifically for our coffee cakes. Drier than what you might put on a cobbler or a pie, it adds a nice crunch. It's great for topping sweet quick breads, too.*

4 tablespoons (2 ounces) unsalted butter

1 cup all-purpose flour

3 tablespoons sugar

2 tablespoons (packed) light brown sugar

1¼ teaspoons ground ginger

1 teaspoon ground cinnamon

**1.** In a small saucepan over low heat (or in a small, microwave-safe bowl in a microwave oven), melt the butter and set aside to cool.

**2.** In a medium bowl, whisk the remaining ingredients, breaking up the brown sugar and distributing it throughout the mixture (using your hands works well here, too).

**3.** Add the melted butter to the flour-spice mixture and mix with a fork or a wooden spoon until fully incorporated and clumps form (again, you can mix with your hands, which is our preferred method).

**4.** Unbaked streusel keeps in an airtight container in the freezer for up to 1 month.

# PUMPKIN OLIVE OIL LOAF

*Yield: two 9 x 5-inch loaves*

*When pumpkins are in season, we make all sorts of pumpkin-y and squash-y baked goods. A few years ago, after a bunch of friends asked us to add something pumpkin into our rotation, we came up with this. The earthy olive oil tones in this recipe play nicely against the sweetness of the gourd.*

Softened unsalted butter and all-purpose flour, for preparing the loaf pans

3⅓ cups all-purpose flour

2 teaspoons baking soda

1½ teaspoons salt

1 teaspoon ground nutmeg

1 teaspoon ground cinnamon

1 teaspoon ground cloves

1 teaspoon ground ginger

½ cup (4 ounces) unsalted butter

3 cups sugar

2 cups pumpkin puree, canned or homemade (see recipe on page 48)

⅔ cup water

½ cup olive oil

4 large eggs, at room temperature

Raw *pepitas* (pumpkin seeds) and turbinado sugar, for garnish

**1.** Preheat the oven to 350°F. Grease two 9 x 5-inch loaf pans with softened butter and dust the pan with flour.

**2.** In a medium bowl, combine the flour, baking soda, salt and all the spices. Set aside.

**3.** In a small saucepan over low heat (or in a small, microwave-safe bowl in a microwave oven), melt the butter and set aside to cool.

**4.** In the bowl of a stand mixer fitted with a paddle attachment (or using a hand mixer), blend the sugar, pumpkin puree, water, olive oil and melted butter until smooth. With the mixer on medium-low, add the eggs, 1 at a time, and mix until well combined.

**5.** Add the flour mixture in 3 batches, mixing on low speed to combine between additions. After the third addition, mix for 15 seconds to ensure the batter is smooth and homogenous so that no flour bits are remaining in the bottom of the bowl.

**6.** Split the batter evenly between the 2 prepared loaf pans. Top with the *pepitas* and turbinado sugar.

**7.** Bake for 60 to 65 minutes, or until a toothpick inserted in the center of the loaf comes out clean.

# PUMPKIN PUREE

*Yield: about 3 cups*

*If you have the time, we recommend making your own pumpkin puree. Any leftovers can be used in pies or even added to savory dishes, like pasta with fresh sage and brown butter—a classic.*

Aluminum foil, for lining the rimmed sheet pan

1 tablespoon canola, safflower or grape seed oil, or another high-smoke-point oil, for greasing the aluminum foil

2 small (about 2 pounds each) whole pie pumpkins (purchase these at your local farmers' market or grocery store; these are sweeter than carving pumpkins)

**1.** Preheat the oven to 350°F. Cover a rimmed sheet pan with aluminum foil and lightly oil the foil.

**2.** Using a very sharp knife, cut off the pumpkin stems, and then cut each pumpkin in half. Scrape out the seeds and wet pulp and set the seeds aside. (We love to clean the seeds, then add oil and salt and bake them.) Be sure all the seeds and wet pulp have been removed.

**3.** Place the pumpkin halves facedown on the prepared sheet pan. Bake for 45 to 50 minutes, or until the skin is easily punctured with a fork.

**4.** Let the pumpkin cool, and then use a spoon to scrape the softened flesh from the pumpkin peel. Using a potato masher or a food processor, mash or pulse the pumpkin until it is smooth. If the puree seems dry, add water a little bit at a time until it is smooth.

**5.** Use immediately or freeze in an airtight container for later use. Puree will keep in a freezer for up to 1 month.

# SAVORY SEED BREAD

*Yield: one 9 x 5-inch loaf*

*This is one of the easiest all-purpose bread recipes you may ever encounter. Our favorite way to eat it is slathered with farmer cheese or* labne, *drizzled with olive oil, and finished off with a pinch of chopped fresh thyme, flaky Maldon sea salt, sumac and freshly cracked pepper.*

Canola oil or nonstick cooking spray, for greasing the loaf pan

¼ cup + 1 teaspoon white sesame seeds

2 tablespoons + 1 teaspoon black caraway (nigella) seeds

2 cups stone-ground spelt flour

2 cups whole-wheat pastry flour

1½ teaspoons baking powder

1½ teaspoons baking soda

1 teaspoon salt

1½ cups whole milk, at room temperature

¾ cup buttermilk, at room temperature

2 tablespoons honey

2 tablespoons extra virgin olive oil

**1.** Preheat the oven to 350°F. Grease a 9 x 5-inch loaf pan with canola oil or nonstick cooking spray.

**2.** Toast the sesame seeds on an unlined rimmed sheet pan for 8 to 10 minutes, or until fragrant. Let cool.

**3.** In a large bowl, whisk together ¼ cup of the sesame seeds, 2 tablespoons of the black caraway seeds, spelt flour, whole-wheat pastry flour, baking powder, baking soda and salt.

**4.** In a separate large bowl, whisk together the whole milk, buttermilk, honey and extra virgin olive oil. Whisk until the honey is completely dissolved, about 45 seconds.

**5.** Add the flour mixture to the milk mixture and mix with a spatula until the batter is just combined.

**6.** Pour the batter into the prepared loaf pan and smooth out the top with a spatula. Sprinkle the top of the batter with the remaining 1 teaspoon sesame seeds and 1 teaspoon black caraway seeds. Bake for 60 to 65 minutes, or until golden and a toothpick inserted in the center of the bread comes out clean.

**7.** Let the bread cool completely before removing it from the pan and slicing.

# SALTED APPLE BREAD

*Yield: one 9 x 5-inch loaf*

*After making our Thanksgiving pies last year, we found ourselves overwhelmed with tons of extra apples, so we decided to cut them into chunks and freeze them for other recipes, like this one. The Salted Breadcrumb Topping adds a bit of savory to this lightly sweetened batter.*

Softened unsalted butter and flour, for preparing the loaf pan

½ cup (4 ounces) unsalted butter

¾ cup whole milk

¾ cup sugar

2 large eggs, at room temperature

¼ cup maple syrup (the darker the better; we use Grade B)

¼ cup hazelnut oil (or substitute ¼ cup canola oil)

½ teaspoon vanilla extract

2 cups all-purpose flour

1 cup rolled oats

½ cup whole-wheat pastry flour

1½ teaspoons ground cinnamon

1 teaspoon baking soda

1 teaspoon baking powder

1 teaspoon salt

¼ teaspoon ground cloves

¼ teaspoon ground nutmeg

1½ cups (7 ounces) peeled, cored and cubed (into ½-inch pieces) apples

Salted Breadcrumb Topping (see inset)

**1.** Preheat the oven to 375°F. Grease a 9 x 5-inch loaf pan with softened butter and dust the pan with flour.

**2.** In a small saucepan over low heat (or in a small, microwave-safe bowl in a microwave oven), melt the butter and set aside to cool.

**3.** In a large bowl, whisk together the whole milk, sugar, eggs, maple syrup, oil, vanilla extract and melted butter until well blended.

**4.** In a separate large bowl, whisk together the all-purpose flour, oats, whole-wheat pastry flour, cinnamon, baking soda, baking powder, salt, cloves and nutmeg.

**5.** Using a spatula or a wooden spoon, add the flour-oat mixture to the milk mixture until almost combined. Fold in the apples until the ingredients are just wet, and the fruit is distributed throughout the batter.

**6.** Pour the batter into the prepared loaf pan and top with the Salted Breadcrumb Topping.

**7.** Bake for 50 to 55 minutes, or until a toothpick inserted in the center of the bread comes out clean.

## SALTED BREADCRUMB TOPPING

*Yield: topping for one loaf*

1 tablespoon unsalted butter

½ cup breadcrumbs, homemade or store-bought

½ teaspoon salt

**1.** In a small saucepan, melt the butter over medium-low heat.

**2.** Add the breadcrumbs and salt, and stir continuously until the breadcrumbs are golden and fragrant, 5 to 7 minutes.

# WHOLE WHEAT BANANA BREAD
## (Adapted from the *Moosewood Cookbook*)

*Yield: one 9 x 5-inch loaf*

*Agatha and I were both vegetarians in high school and college, and for both of us, Mollie Katzen's* Moosewood Cookbook *was our bible. This recipe is an altered version of hers and utilizes maple syrup and sour cream for moistness and flaxseed for earthiness. It's one of the few recipes I've committed to heart—I've made it that many times. Try it toasted and smothered with thick, unsweetened Greek yogurt for breakfast.*

Canola oil or nonstick cooking spray, for greasing the loaf pan

2 large ripe bananas (to make 1 cup of mashed)

¼ cup whole flaxseeds

¾ cup all-purpose flour

¾ cup whole-wheat flour

1 tablespoon baking powder

½ tablespoon baking soda

½ teaspoon salt

½ cup maple syrup (the darker the better; we use Grade B)

2 large eggs, at room temperature

⅓ cup canola oil

¼ cup (packed) light brown sugar

1 teaspoon vanilla extract

⅓ cup sour cream (preferably full-fat)

1. Preheat the oven to 350°F. Liberally grease a 9 x 5-inch loaf pan with canola oil or nonstick cooking spray.

2. Peel the bananas and place them in a small bowl. Using the back of a fork, mash them until smooth. Separate out 1 cup of the banana mash. If there is extra, you can freeze it in an airtight container for later use, or purpose it for another recipe (or even add it to yogurt or oatmeal for breakfast).

3. Grind the flaxseeds into a fine powder using a coffee or spice grinder. (Store-bought flaxseed meal works, too.)

4. In a medium bowl, whisk together the flours, flaxseed meal, baking powder, baking soda and salt. Set aside.

5. In a large bowl, whisk together the maple syrup, eggs, canola oil, light brown sugar and vanilla extract. Add the sour cream and the mashed bananas. Whisk until almost smooth and only a few lumps remain.

6. Fold the dry ingredients into the wet ingredients until just combined. Do not overmix.

7. Pour the batter into the prepared loaf pan. Bake on the middle rack in the oven for 50 to 55 minutes, or until a toothpick inserted in the center of the bread comes out clean.

# MUFFINS

*Agatha* ❖ I am a firm believer in eating first thing in the morning. I'd like to say that I do it to feel balanced throughout the day or because it gives my skin a healthy glow. But the truth is that I simply wake up starving every morning. For me, the first bite of food I put in my mouth on any given day pretty much sets the tone for how the rest of the day will unfold.

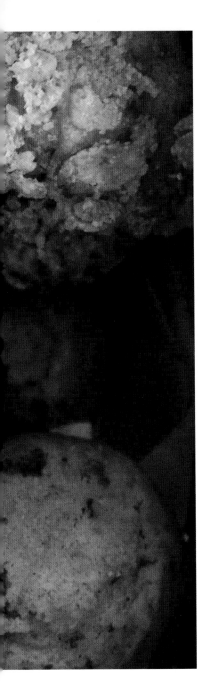

There are people who like variation in their first meal, and there are those who are creatures of habit, who *need* the same blueberry muffin and iced coffee every morning. And by that, I mean *every single morning*. If we sell out of our Blueberry Cornflake Muffins just as such a customer arrives, she will groan and depart empty-handed and grumpy. But, no doubt, she'll be back the following day, ready for her daily fix.

I respect that type of ritual and loyalty. There is something comforting about a breakfast routine, which is why we work around the clock at Ovenly to try to satisfy our customers' morning cravings. We like to think that we are providing a happy break on a tough day in the big city.

When Erin and I first started baking together, muffins were not on our radar. We were used to seeing the giant, bland chocolate chip–studded mounds wrapped in plastic and sold at the corner bodega, which didn't really appeal to us. But when tons of muffin requests started coming in from our clients, we decided to take a shot at creating muffins that were less predictable and more fun (and not so huge). We experimented for weeks—living, breathing and eating muffins—until we were sick. And then we started to get excited. The more flavor combinations we came up with, the more room we found in our hearts (and stomachs) for muffins. We soon realized that the best muffins are simple ones, and when made with flavorful ingredients, they are damn good.

If you've got a standard set of baking ingredients handy—flour, eggs, butter, sugar, leavening and salt—and 30 minutes to spare, you are ready to conquer these recipes. Unlike with scones, precision isn't so important with muffins. As long as you keep in mind the cardinal rule—"Do not overmix the batter"—the baking gods will be on your side. Once you decide on a base recipe, you can switch up the fillings and the sizes, making the muffins savory or sweet, extra-large or miniature and cute. Go ahead and top them with turbinado sugar, a crumble or a smear of butter. In a party pinch, top them with buttercream and call them cupcakes. Magic!

While our recipes are fairly straightforward, the bakers at Ovenly can attest to the fact that mistakes do happen. So after a few near disasters, our motto is "There are no failures in muffin making." (Refer to the Muffin Bread Pudding recipe on page 70 for proof.)

# BLUEBERRY CORNFLAKE MUFFINS

*Yield: 12 muffins*

*As a kid, I relished scarfing down giant bowls of cornflakes with fresh blueberries. Sometimes when I was feeling naughty, I would toss on a few (like, five) extra spoonfuls of sugar when my dad wasn't looking. This recipe is our version of a breakfast cereal in muffin form. Since Erin and I are all grown up now, we've cut out spoonfuls of sugar and made this recipe palatable for adults. Rest assured, kids will go crazy over them, too.*

Softened unsalted butter or nonstick cooking spray or 12 baking cups, for greasing or lining the muffin tin

1½ cups all-purpose flour

1½ teaspoons baking powder

¼ teaspoon baking soda

¼ teaspoon salt

1 cup blueberries (fresh or frozen)

½ cup sugar

6 tablespoons (3 ounces) unsalted butter, at room temperature

¾ cup sour cream (preferably full-fat)

1 large egg, at room temperature

1 teaspoon vanilla extract

Zest of 1 lemon

Cornflake Topping (see inset)

**1.** Preheat the oven to 350°F. Grease the wells of a 12-cup muffin tin with softened butter or nonstick cooking spray, or use baking cups.

**2.** In a medium bowl, whisk together the flour, baking powder, baking soda and salt. Reserve ¼ cup of the flour mixture. In a small bowl, coat the blueberries evenly with the reserved flour mixture. Set aside.

**3.** In the bowl of a stand mixer fitted with a paddle attachment (or using a hand mixer), cream the sugar and butter on medium-high speed until the mixture is smooth and light yellow, about 2 minutes.

**4.** Turn the mixer off and add the sour cream, egg, vanilla extract and lemon zest. Beat on medium-low speed until smooth, about 30 seconds. Scrape down the sides and the bottom of the bowl, using a rubber spatula. Mix again for an additional 5 seconds.

**5.** Add the flour mixture to the wet mixture and mix on low speed until just combined, about 15 seconds. Remove the bowl from the stand mixer.

**6.** Using a spatula, gently fold the coated blueberries into the batter.

**7.** Portion out the batter into the wells of the prepared muffin tin, using a large spoon or a cookie scoop. Fill each well about ⅔ full.

**8.** Top each muffin with 2 tablespoons Cornflake Topping. Bake for 25 to 28 minutes, or until a toothpick inserted in the center of a few muffins comes out clean.

## CORNFLAKE TOPPING
### (see process on page 60)

*Yield: topping for 12 muffins*

1 cup cornflakes (organic or without high fructose corn syrup)

¼ cup (4 tablespoons) unsalted butter, at room temperature

¼ cup turbinado sugar

**1.** Cut the butter into ¼ to ½-inch cubes.

**2.** In a small bowl, combine all the ingredients.

**3.** Mix with your hands or a wooden spoon until the cornflakes, butter and sugar are well combined and there are no butter chunks. The cornflakes should be slightly crushed.

## CORNFLAKE TOPPING PROCESS

01   Gather all the ingredients, measure each into its own small bowl (in our bakery, we call this creating a *mise en place*) and cut the butter into cubes.

02   In a small bowl, combine all the ingredients.

03   Use your hands (or a wooden spoon) to mix everything together, slightly crushing the cornflakes.

04   Ensure that the butter is well incorporated into the mixture and that no large pieces remain.

*We avoid using ingredients that contain high fructose corn syrup.*
*You may have noticed that many cereals contain it, so try to find an organic*
*version of cornflakes, or be sure to read ingredients labels on cereal boxes.*

# CHEDDAR CORN MUFFINS

*Yield: 12 muffins*

*Dale Goldberg, one of our first bakers at Ovenly, invented this recipe while we were on a company mission to develop a corn flour–based savory option for our menu. It's an unassuming muffin that packs a ton of flavor. Topped with sharp white cheddar, which adds color to the bright golden crust, and featuring cumin and ancho chile powder, this recipe results in a marriage of robust flavors.*

Softened unsalted butter or nonstick cooking spray or 12 baking cups, for greasing or lining the muffin tin

2 cups all-purpose flour

¾ cup sugar

½ cup + 2 tablespoons medium ground, yellow cornmeal

2 teaspoons salt

1½ teaspoons baking powder

1½ teaspoons freshly ground black pepper

1½ teaspoons ground cumin

½ teaspoon garlic powder

¼ teaspoon baking soda

2 large eggs, at room temperature

⅔ cup sour cream (preferably full-fat)

⅔ cup buttermilk

⅓ cup canola oil

1¼ cups shredded sharp white cheddar, plus extra shredded cheddar for garnish

Ancho chile powder, for garnish

1. Preheat the oven to 350°F. Grease the wells of a 12-cup muffin tin with softened butter or nonstick cooking spray, or use baking cups.

2. In a large bowl, whisk together all the dry ingredients.

3. In a separate large bowl, whisk the eggs until smooth, and then whisk in the sour cream, buttermilk and canola oil until smooth and fully incorporated.

4. Add the flour mixture to the wet mixture. Using a wooden spoon or a large spatula, stir together until just incorporated.

5. Add the cheddar and incorporate it fully into the batter.

6. Portion out the batter into the wells of the prepared muffin tin, using a large spoon or a cookie scoop. Fill each well about ⅔ full.

7. Top each muffin generously with the remaining shredded cheddar, and sprinkle with a pinch of ancho chile powder.

8. Bake for 22 to 24 minutes, or until a toothpick inserted in the center of a few muffins comes out clean.

*Tip*

*Get adventurous with these muffins by substituting blue cheese for the white cheddar for a spicier, piquant flavor.*

# CURRANT WALNUT CRUMBLE MUFFINS

*Yield: 12 muffins*

Softened unsalted butter or
nonstick cooking spray or
12 baking cups, for greasing
or lining the muffin tin

½ cup chopped walnuts

10 tablespoons (5 ounces)
unsalted butter

2 cups all-purpose flour

1 tablespoon baking powder

1 teaspoon ground cinnamon

½ teaspoon salt

1 cup dried currants

½ cup (packed) light brown sugar

¼ cup + 2 tablespoons sugar

2 large eggs, at room temperature

¾ cup sour cream
(preferably full-fat)

2 teaspoons (packed) lemon zest

1 teaspoon vanilla extract

Oat Walnut Streusel
(see inset)

**1.** Preheat the oven to 350°F. Grease the wells of a 12-cup muffin tin with softened butter or nonstick cooking spray, or use baking cups.

**2.** Toast the walnuts on a rimmed sheet pan in the oven for about 10 minutes, or until golden and fragrant.

**3.** In a small saucepan over low heat or in a small, microwave-safe bowl in a microwave oven, melt the butter and set aside to cool.

**4.** In a medium bowl, whisk together the flour, baking powder, cinnamon and salt. Mix in the currants and the toasted walnuts. Set aside.

**5.** In the bowl of a stand mixer fitted with a paddle attachment (or using a hand mixer), beat together the sugars and the melted butter on medium-high speed until smooth, about 1 minute. The mixture will resemble thick caramel.

**6.** Break the eggs into a small bowl, and beat them lightly with a fork, breaking the yolks. With the mixer on medium-high speed, add the eggs and then beat until the batter is light and fluffy, about 3 minutes. Scrape down the sides of the bowl and mix on medium speed for 10 more seconds. With the mixer off, add the sour cream, lemon zest and vanilla extract. Beat on medium speed until just combined, about 30 seconds.

---

### OAT WALNUT STREUSEL

*Yield: topping for 12 muffins*

3 tablespoons (1½ ounces)
unsalted butter
½ cup all-purpose flour
¼ cup rolled oats
¼ cup sugar
2 tablespoons chopped
toasted walnuts
¼ teaspoon salt

**1.** In a small saucepan over low heat (or in a small, microwave-safe bowl in a microwave oven), melt the butter and set aside to cool.

**2.** In a medium bowl, stir together the flour, oats, sugar, walnuts and salt. Pour the melted butter into the bowl, and then stir the mixture with a spatula until fully combined and crumbs form.

**3.** Streusel can be made ahead and frozen for up to one month.

---

**7.** Turn the mixer off, and add the flour mixture. Mix on low speed until just combined. Do not overmix.

**8.** Portion out the batter into the wells of the prepared muffin tin, using a large spoon or a cookie scoop. Fill each well about ²/₃ full.

**9.** Top each muffin generously with the Oat Walnut Streusel. Bake for 20 to 24 minutes, or until a toothpick inserted in the center of a few muffins comes out clean.

# FETA, BASIL & SCALLION MUFFINS

*Yield: 12 muffins*

*When we started offering winter soup specials at our café (Erin is our soup maker extraordinaire), we went on a mission to come up with a savory muffin that could accompany the soups. Since Erin and I are both serious fromage lovers (I dream of getting lost in cheese caves), whatever we came up with was destined to be cheesy. We experimented with a few different cheeses and tossed in a variety of herbs from our neighbors over at Eagle Street Rooftop Farm. After reworking the recipe a few times, we nailed it: feta, fresh basil and chopped scallions. The combination proved to be the salty and earthy flavor we were looking for.*

Softened unsalted butter or nonstick cooking spray or 12 baking cups, for greasing or lining the muffin tin

2 cups all-purpose flour

1 tablespoon sugar

1 tablespoon baking powder

1¼ teaspoons paprika

½ teaspoon garlic powder

¼ teaspoon salt

1 cup (8 ounces) crumbled feta

4 scallions, washed, root ends trimmed and finely chopped

8 fresh basil leaves, chopped into thin strips

¾ cup whole milk

½ cup canola oil

2 large eggs, at room temperature

Maldon sea salt, paprika and red pepper flakes, for garnish

**1.** Preheat the oven to 350°F. Grease the wells of a 12-cup muffin tin with softened butter or nonstick cooking spray, or use baking cups.

**2.** In a large bowl, whisk together the flour, sugar, baking powder, spices and salt. Whisk in the feta, scallions and basil. Set aside.

**3.** In a separate large bowl, whisk together the whole milk, canola oil and eggs until smooth.

**4.** Add the flour mixture to the milk-egg mixture. Using a wooden spoon or large spatula, stir together until just combined.

**5.** Portion out the batter into the wells of the prepared muffin tin, using a large spoon or a cookie scoop. Fill each well about ¾ full.

**6.** Sprinkle the tops of each muffin with a pinch of Maldon sea salt, paprika and red pepper flakes. Bake for about 20 minutes, or until a toothpick inserted in the center of a few muffins comes out clean.

- - - - - - - - - - - - - - - - - - - - - - - - - - - - - - - -

*In your quest to make your own perfect savory muffin, try experimenting with different cheeses, herbs and spices. This recipe is versatile and adaptable to whatever ingredients you have on hand and to seasonal fresh herbs. Mozzarella will ooze beautifully out of this muffin; fall-fresh rosemary can be substituted for summer basil. Or try reducing the salt and throw in some smoky bacon leftover from breakfast instead.*

- - - - - - - - - - - - - - - - - - - - - - - - - - - - - - - -

# HARVEST MUFFINS

## *Yield: 20 muffins*

*I like to think of the Morning Glory as the 1970s love-child muffin. The marriage of fruits and vegetables combined with whole-grain flours resulted in a hearty treat for the heart-healthy masses, and you can still find the muffins in most corner bakeries today. Problem is, the Morning Glory is usually overly sweet and made with the wrong combinations of whole-wheat and all-purpose flour, which gives it a gritty texture. Sadly, people now tend to associate that grit with "healthy" baked goods. The glorious Harvest Muffin, our riff on the classic Morning Glory, challenges that perception. We add in our favorite spelt flour from Daisy Organic Flours, which gives this muffin a supersoft, nutty texture that is unbeatable.*

Softened unsalted butter or nonstick spray or 20 baking cups, for greasing or lining the muffin tins

8 tablespoons (4 ounces) unsalted butter

2 cups spelt flour (preferably Daisy Organic Flours brand, if available)

1½ cups all-purpose flour

1 cup (packed) dark brown sugar

⅔ cup sugar

½ cup wheat bran

2 teaspoons salt

2 teaspoons baking powder

1 teaspoon baking soda

1 tablespoon ground cinnamon

1½ teaspoons ground ginger

½ teaspoon ground cardamom

2 cups grated carrots

1 cup unsweetened shredded coconut

1 cup dried currants (or seedless black raisins)

2 cups buttermilk

2 large eggs, at room temperature

**1.** Preheat the oven to 350°F. Grease the wells of two 12-cup muffin tins with softened butter or nonstick cooking spray, or use baking cups.

**2.** In a small saucepan over low heat (or in a small, microwave-safe bowl in a microwave oven), melt the butter and set aside to cool.

**3.** In a large bowl, whisk together spelt flour, all-purpose flour, sugars, wheat bran, salt, baking powder, baking soda, cinnamon, ginger and cardamom. Then stir in the carrots, coconut and currants.

**4.** In a separate large bowl, whisk the buttermilk into the melted butter. Add the eggs and whisk together until well combined.

**5.** Add the carrot-flour mixture to the buttermilk mixture and mix until combined.

**6.** Portion out the batter into the wells of the prepared muffin tins, using a large spoon or a cookie scoop. Fill each well about ⅔ full.

**7.** Bake for 25 to 28 minutes, or until a toothpick inserted in the center of a few muffins comes out clean.

# JELLY DOUGHNUT MUFFINS

*Yield: 12 muffins*

*When we were craving doughnuts but making muffins, we realized that the in-between was a cinnamon-sugar batter filled with our homemade blueberry jam. A doughnut, but a muffin, too!*

Softened unsalted butter or nonstick cooking spray or 12 baking cups, for greasing or lining the muffin tin

2 cups all-purpose flour

1½ teaspoons baking powder

1 teaspoon ground nutmeg

1 teaspoon ground cinnamon

½ teaspoon salt

¾ cup sugar

¼ cup canola oil

1 large egg, at room temperature

¾ cup whole milk

¼ cup + 2 tablespoons jam of your choice, for filling

¼ cup (4 tablespoons) unsalted butter, for brushing

⅓ cup sugar

1 tablespoon ground cinnamon

**1.** Preheat the oven to 350°F. Grease the wells of a 12-cup muffin tin with softened butter or nonstick cooking spray, or use baking cups.

**2.** In a medium bowl, whisk together the flour, baking powder, spices and salt. Set aside.

**3.** In a large bowl, whisk together the sugar, canola oil and egg. Add the whole milk and whisk until smooth.

**4.** Add the flour mixture to the egg mixture and stir with a spatula until just combined.

**5.** Using a scoop or a spoon, fill each muffin tin well with 2 tablespoons of batter (you can eyeball it). Spoon 1½ teaspoons jam onto the very center of the batter (it should not touch the sides of the muffin tin well), and then top with another 2 tablespoons of batter. Repeat until all the wells have been filled.

**6.** Bake for 22 to 24 minutes, or until a toothpick inserted in the center of a few muffins comes out clean.

**7.** Five minutes before the muffins are done baking, in a small saucepan over low heat or in a small, microwave-safe bowl in a microwave oven, melt the butter and set aside to cool. In a small bowl, combine the sugar and cinnamon. Set aside.

**8.** Remove the muffins from the oven and let cool for 5 minutes. Dip the top of each warm muffin into the melted butter, and then lightly dip it into the cinnamon-sugar topping, coating each muffin evenly.

**9.** Let cool and serve.

# MUFFIN BREAD PUDDING

*Yield: one 13 x 9-inch pan*

*We've come to realize that assessing someone's baking prowess is based not only on the person's ability to breeze through a recipe gracefully, but also on the person's ability to transform a complete baking disaster into a mouthwatering masterpiece. Among our bakers, Laura Russell was the crafty conjurer who continually performed such feats. Coffee cake batter made with three times as many eggs as the recipe called for? She transformed it into fluffy "pancakes," which we feasted on for family meal. Forty pounds of muffin batter sans sugar (whoops!)? The café special became an unbelievably delicious "bread pudding" topped with cream cheese icing. In every blundered recipe there is a culinary creation waiting to be discovered.*

Softened unsalted butter and all-purpose flour, for preparing the baking pan

1 pound leftover muffins (or the bready ingredient of choice)

3 cups whole milk

3 cups heavy cream

1 cup sugar

8 large eggs, at room temperature

1 teaspoon vanilla extract

Aluminum foil, for covering the baking pan

Cream Cheese Icing (see inset)

**1.** Preheat the oven to 375°F. Grease a 13 x 9-inch baking pan with softened butter and dust with flour.

**2.** Tear or cut the leftover muffins into 1-inch pieces or cubes. Layer the pieces evenly over the bottom of the prepared baking pan.

**3.** In a large saucepan over medium heat, bring the whole milk, heavy cream and sugar to a boil. Remove from the heat and let cool for 5 minutes.

**4.** In a small bowl, whisk together the eggs and vanilla extract, and then add to the cooled milk mixture, whisking until smooth. Pour the milk-egg mixture over the muffin pieces in the baking pan. Let soak for 30 minutes in the refrigerator.

**5.** Cover the pan with aluminum foil and bake for 45 to 50 minutes. Take the pan out of the oven, and then carefully remove the foil. Touch the top of the bread pudding to test for doneness. If it bounces back and no batter sticks to your finger, then it is done.

**6.** Let the bread pudding cool fully, and then top with Cream Cheese Icing before serving.

## CREAM CHEESE ICING

*Yield: icing for 1 pan of Muffin Bread Pudding*

¾ cup (6 ounces) cream cheese, softened
½ cup confectioners' sugar, sifted
¼ teaspoon ground cinnamon
¼ whole milk
1 teaspoon vanilla extract

**1.** In the bowl of a stand mixer fitted with a paddle attachment (or using a hand mixer), whip the cream cheese, confectioners' sugar and cinnamon on medium-high until light and fluffy, about 3 minutes.

**2.** With the machine on low, add the whole milk and vanilla extract and mix until smooth, about 1 minute more.

# COOKIES &
# SHORTBREADS

*Erin* ❖ In the spring of 2011, we moved from Paulie Gee's windowless kitchen in industrial Greenpoint, Brooklyn, to another windowless commercial kitchen in even more industrial Red Hook. At 4:00 a.m. Commerce Street feels like a manufacturing wasteland, and when we pulled up for our first predawn baking shift, Agatha and I questioned what we were thinking moving to such a desolate (and sort of scary) place.

But then the sun came up, and while Agatha made deliveries, I took my first walk around the neighborhood. I found that those seemingly ominous cinder-block facades actually housed humming businesses. I headed down the block toward the East River and saw that the roastery and packing house for Stumptown Coffee Roasters occupied a loft factory space on the corner. I walked in and, over the loud hum of the stories-tall mid-twentieth-century Probat, attempted to introduce myself to a prominently tattooed, muscular guy who wore noise-canceling headphones. He periodically removed a small tube of beans from a large metal cylinder attached to the massive machine, and smelled them as they churned through the inner workings of the roaster. After signaling to me that I should wait a couple of minutes, he pulled a lever that sent hundreds of pounds of coffee beans into a drum with an explosion of heat and steam. He removed his ear protection and introduced himself.

Steve Kirbach, head roaster for Stumptown Coffee Roasters, was finishing up a year in New York City after training the company's local staff. He graciously gave me a tour of the space, introduced me to his (adorable, also tattooed and mostly male) colleagues, and loaded my arms with beans, branded mugs and other Stumptown swag. Later in the day, Agatha and I returned the favor and brought over a whole mess of treats. It was the beginning of a beautiful relationship.

A few months later, an agonizing heat wave hit New York City. Our kitchen was barely ventilated, and we watched in horror as the thermometer affixed to the wall climbed to 105, 108, then 114 degrees. It was so hot that we had to work inside of our sputtering walk-in refrigerator, scooping cookie dough in the small, cold space to prevent it from melting. We even considered working in bikinis but nixed that idea when we imagined the types of burns we could get from bumping into our blistering ovens (ouch). Our new friends down the block, knowing how we were suffering, provided us with a steady supply of cold brew to keep us caffeinated and cooled.

When the heat passed, Agatha and I showed our appreciation by creating a coffee bean–infused treat for the Stumptown boys. We argued and tinkered and tested. I was content with using just a dash of espresso in the recipe, but Agatha wasn't totally satisfied. She wanted to add cardamom to mimic the coffee traditions of the Middle East. I wanted to add more sugar. I always want to add more sugar. Agatha thought it was too sweet to begin with. We played a long game of culinary tug-of-war until finally our espresso–burnt sugar shortbread was born. Called The Stumptown Shorty (see recipe on page 91), it's your favorite cup of coffee in cookie form.

Since my palate sensibilities tend to be more traditional and sweet, and Agatha's more unorthodox and savory, there's usually a friendly and spirited argument about which spices and flavors to include in our baked goods. For example, I required that Agatha's moist mustard cookie had to be tempered with additions of earthy clove and molasses-loaded dark brown sugar, while Agatha insisted that my hazelnut cookie be enlivened with orange zest and maple syrup. Each of the recipes in this chapter represents our signature balance of sweet, savory and spice. And none of them are predictable—just like those unexpected moments and serendipitous encounters throughout Ovenly's history.

Before delving in, we extend our sincerest apologies to you crispy cookie lovers out there: despite our debates on flavor, Agatha and I both prefer a cookie that is soft and chewy, or buttery and tender. If you're in our camp, you're about to be in cookie heaven.

# SALTED CHOCOLATE CHIP COOKIES

*Yield: approximately 18 cookies*

*After finishing college, I packed up my liberal arts degree and started work as a waitress at a vegetarian diner (I was an aspiring actor back then, and that's what us theater majors do). The owners of the restaurant were a kooky husband-and-wife team whose hearts and wardrobe had never left the 1960s, and the chef was an enormous man adept at backhanded compliments. "Honey, I hear you like to bake. I bet you're good at it! Bring in something next time you make it. And—as a favor to you—I'll improve anything you bring me." Those were fighting words. The diner made vegan chocolate chip cookies that were the type of dessert that gave "vegan" a bad rap. I decided that I would create a vegan cookie that put the restaurant's version to shame. Little did I know that eight years later, Agatha would take that ancient recipe and alter it to make it absolutely perfect. We're not talking the perfect vegan chocolate chip cookie. We're talking the perfect chocolate chip cookie. Period. The recipe for this cookie (which, by far, is our best selling item) is very specific and needs to be followed to a T. Trust us, if you follow the rules, you'll be ecstatic about the results.*

2 cups all-purpose flour

1 teaspoon baking powder

¾ teaspoon baking soda

½ teaspoon salt

1¼ cups dark chocolate chips*

½ cup sugar

½ cup (packed) light brown sugar

½ cup + 1 tablespoon canola oil

¼ cup + 1 tablespoon water

Coarse-grained sea salt or flaky sea salt like Maldon, for garnish

*\*We prefer chocolate with 60 percent cocoa content or higher.*

**1.** In a large bowl, whisk together the flour, baking powder, baking soda and salt. Add the chocolate chips to the flour mixture, and toss to coat.

**2.** In a separate large bowl, whisk the sugars briskly with the canola oil and water until smooth and incorporated, about 2 minutes. Note: use fresh, soft light brown sugar. If there are clumps, break them up with the back of a spoon or your hand before whisking.

**3.** Add the flour mixture to the sugar mixture, and then stir with a wooden spoon or a rubber spatula until just combined and no flour is visible. Do not overmix.

**4.** Cover with plastic wrap. Refrigerate the dough for at least 12 hours and up to 24 hours. Do not skip this step.

**5.** Preheat the oven to 350°F. Line a rimmed sheet pan with parchment paper.

**6.** Remove dough from the refrigerator and use a scoop or a spoon to form the cold dough into approximately 1½-inch (1½- to 1¾-ounce) balls and place them on the prepared rimmed sheet pan. If using a scoop, pack the dough into the scoop to make dense pucks. We recommend freezing the balls of dough for 10 minutes before baking as the cookies will retain their shape better that way while baking.

**7.** Sprinkle the balls of dough with coarse-grained sea salt (if freezing, remove balls of dough from the freezer first), and bake for 12 to 13 minutes, or until the edges are just golden. Do not overbake.

**8.** Let cool completely before serving.

# PEANUT BUTTER COOKIES

## (Inspired by our friend Emmy Tiderington)

### Yield: 12 large cookies; 24 small cookies

*When Agatha and I first started to develop gluten-free baked goods, I turned to my friend Emmy Tiderington, who has a wheat allergy, for inspiration. We have Emmy to thank for the recipe that would act as a stepping-stone for our own gluten-free peanut butter cookie. Dense and deeply nutty, this peanut butter cookie is also perfectly chewy. The crunchy salt topping provides a balance to the brown sugar and sweet vanilla. As a variation, try Emmy's original by substituting the Skippy with a 16-ounce jar of all-natural peanut butter, trading out the brown sugar for 1 cup of honey and omitting the vanilla.*

---

1¾ cups (packed) light brown sugar

2 large eggs, at room temperature

½ teaspoon vanilla extract

1¾ cups peanut butter*

Coarse-grained sea salt,
for garnish

*\*While the all-natural stuff works just fine for this cookie, Skippy is our peanut butter brand of choice for this recipe as we've found the dough retains its shape best with it.*

**1.** Preheat the oven to 350°F. Line a rimmed sheet pan with parchment paper.

**2.** In a medium bowl, vigorously whisk together the light brown sugar and eggs until incorporated. Whisk in the vanilla extract. Add the peanut butter and mix with a spatula until smooth and completely incorporated, and until no ribbons of peanut butter can be seen. You know the dough is ready when it is the consistency of Play-Doh.

**3.** Using a scoop or a spoon, form the dough into twelve approximately 2-inch (2- to 2¼-ounce) balls and place them on the prepared rimmed sheet pan. For smaller cookies, use a heaping tablespoon.

**4.** Sprinkle the dough balls lightly with coarse-grained sea salt just before baking. Bake for 20 to 22 minutes, turning the rimmed sheet pan once halfway through baking (for smaller cookies, bake for 16 to 18 minutes). When finished the cookies will be lightly golden and cracked on top. Let cool completely before serving.

**5.** You can bake these cookies as soon as the dough is prepared, but they will retain their shape better if you freeze them for 15 minutes before baking.

# MUSTARD SPICE COOKIES

*Yield: 24 cookies*

*This traditional chewy ginger cookie, one of our staff's favorites, is spiked with a bit of mustard. Don't let the addition of your favorite hot dog condiment scare you.*

2¼ cups all-purpose flour

3 teaspoons ground ginger

1 teaspoon ground cinnamon

½ teaspoon ground cloves

1 teaspoon baking soda

1 teaspoon salt

1 cup (8 ounces) unsalted butter, at room temperature

1 cup sugar

1 large egg, at room temperature

2 tablespoons molasses

2 tablespoons maple syrup (the darker the better; we prefer Grade B)

2 tablespoons whole-grain mustard (like Tin or Maille)

1 tablespoon heavy cream

Turbinado sugar, for garnish

**1.** In a large bowl, whisk together the flour, ginger, cinnamon, cloves, baking soda and salt. Set aside.

**2.** In the bowl of a stand mixer fitted with a paddle attachment (or using a hand mixer), beat the butter on medium speed for 1 minute. Add the sugar. Beat on medium-high until light and fluffy, about 3 minutes.

**3.** Turn the machine off, and add the egg. Mix on low until just combined.

**4.** With the machine off, add the molasses, maple syrup, mustard and cream and then beat on low until incorporated.

**5.** Again with the machine off, add the flour mixture. Then mix on low until it is completely incorporated, about 30 seconds.

**6.** Remove the bowl from the mixer, and cover with plastic wrap. Refrigerate the dough for at least 1 hour and up to 3 hours before scooping.

**7.** Preheat the oven to 350°F. Line a rimmed sheet pan with parchment paper.

**8.** Using a scoop or spoon, form the dough into 1-inch (1½-ounce) balls and arrange them on the prepared rimmed sheet pans.

**9.** Sprinkle the dough balls with turbinado sugar and bake for 12 minutes, rotating the pan halfway through baking, or until light golden on the edges. Do not over-bake. If the middle appears slightly wet, that is okay. The cookies will set as they cool. Let them cool fully before serving.

*Be sure to scoop all the mustard spice dough the same day that it is made. If you are not going to bake all the dough the same day, freeze it on rimmed sheet pans, and then remove and freeze the dough balls in an airtight container or plastic bag until using. Before baking, let the frozen dough come to room temperature for 10 minutes or so.*

# BOURBON CHOCOLATE CHIP COOKIES WITH TARRAGON

*Yield: 24 cookies*

*When we first visited Colin Spoelman at his Kings County Distillery, we left a little tipsy and with plenty of bourbon. At the time of our visit, we had already been experimenting with a boozy-based cookie, and our new bottles of liquor helped us finalize it. The result was this herby, chocolaty treat. Beware. It packs a real punch!*

1 cup (8 ounces) unsalted butter

2½ cups all-purpose flour

¾ teaspoon baking soda

¾ teaspoon salt

1 cup sugar

¾ cup (packed) light brown sugar

1 large egg, at room temperature

1 large egg yolk

¼ cup bourbon (a cheaper brand for baking is fine)

1 teaspoon vanilla extract

1 cup bittersweet or milk chocolate chips*

1 tablespoon finely chopped fresh tarragon

*\*If bittersweet, we prefer chocolate with 60 percent cocoa content or higher. For milk chocolate, we prefer chocolate with 30–35 percent cocoa content.*

**1.** In a small saucepan over medium-low heat, melt the butter and continue to heat it until it crackles and foams. Once the foam begins to subside, the butter solids will quickly begin to brown on the bottom of the pan. Stir continuously with a wooden spoon to scrape browned bits off the bottom of the saucepan. Once the butter is nutty brown in color, remove it from the heat. Do not let the butter burn. Set aside and let cool. (See the Brown Butter Process on page 133.)

**2.** While the butter cools, in a large bowl, whisk together the flour, baking soda and salt. Set aside.

**3.** In the bowl of a stand mixer fitted with a paddle attachment (or using a hand mixer), beat together cooled melted brown butter and sugars on medium speed until fully incorporated, about 1 minute.

**4.** Place the whole egg and egg yolk in a small bowl. With the mixer on low, add the eggs slowly to the butter mixture. Raise the mixer speed to medium-high, and beat for 1 minute, or until smooth.

**5.** Turn the mixer to low, add the bourbon and vanilla extract, and then beat until combined, about 30 seconds.

**6.** With the mixer on low speed, add the flour mixture and mix until barely incorporated, about 30 seconds. Add the chocolate chips and tarragon, mixing until all the dry ingredients are incorporated, about 30 seconds more.

**7.** Preheat the oven to 350°F. Line two rimmed sheet pans with parchment paper.

**8.** Cover dough with plastic wrap. Chill for 30 minutes. Remove from refrigerator and, using a scoop or a spoon, form the dough into 1-inch (1½-ounce) balls and arrange them on the prepared rimmed sheet pans.

**9.** Bake for 10 minutes, or until light golden. The cookies will look slightly under-baked and soft in the center, but they will set. Let them cool fully before serving.

# CHEWY CHOCOLATE GINGER COOKIES

*Yield: approximately 24 cookies*

3 cups chopped dark chocolate*

2 tablespoons canola oil

1 tablespoon unsalted butter

¾ cup (packed) light brown sugar

4 large eggs, at room temperature

1 teaspoon vanilla extract

1¼ cup all-purpose flour

2 teaspoons baking powder

1½ teaspoons salt

¼ cup minced crystallized ginger**

*\* We prefer chocolate with 70 percent or higher cocoa content for these cookies.*

*\*\* If you are a ginger lover, increase amount to ½ cup.*

**1.** Preheat the oven to 350°F. Line two rimmed sheet pans with parchment paper.

**2.** Place the chocolate, canola oil and butter in a metal bowl. Place the bowl over a saucepan filled with 1 inch of water to create a double boiler. Melt the chocolate with the oil and butter over medium-low heat and let cool fully. (You can also melt the mixture in a microwave-safe bowl by heating in a microwave oven for 20 seconds. After 20 seconds, stir and repeat until fully melted.)

**3.** While chocolate mixture is melting, in a large bowl whisk together the light brown sugar, eggs and vanilla extract until smooth and incorporated.

**4.** Pour the cooled chocolate mixture into the egg mixture, and mix with a rubber spatula or wooden spoon until combined.

**5.** In a separate, small bowl, whisk together the flour, baking powder and salt.

**6.** Add the flour mixture to the chocolate-egg mixture, and mix with a rubber spatula or wooden spoon until almost combined. Add the ginger, and stir until all the ingredients are fully incorporated, and no flour can be seen. The dough will be very gooey.

**7.** Using a scoop or a spoon, form the dough into 2-inch (2-ounce) balls. (If you want perfectly shaped cookies, we recommend refrigerating the dough for 15 minutes before scooping onto prepared pans.) Bake for 12 to 13 minutes, or until cracks form on the top of the cookies and they look just set. Let them cool fully before serving.

## Get Creative

Instead of using crystallized ginger, use the same amount of chopped, dried fruit or chopped, toasted nuts. You can also omit the ginger completely. This cookie is also delicious topped with crushed pink peppercorns.

We like to scoop all our doughs onto rimmed sheet pans, freeze them for 30 minutes, then transfer the dough balls to ziplock bags to store in the freezer. This way, we always have fresh treats ready to bake for any unexpected guests or cookie cravings. Be sure to add a few extra minutes to the baking time for cookies that are baked from frozen.

# HAZELNUT MAPLE COOKIES WITH ORANGE ZEST

*Yield: approximately 24 cookies*

*When I studied abroad, I lived and traveled on a fraying shoestring budget, which meant that most of my money went to train tickets and basic foods: bread, cheese and kalimotxo (aka cocavino)—Coca-Cola mixed with cheap red wine. When I arrived in Italy, however, my college appetite was delighted to discover that there were some amazing affordable baked goods. One of my favorites was a little pistachio cookie made only with nuts, egg whites, sugar and lemon zest. This is our version of that simple biscotto.*

1 pound raw hazelnuts, plus 12 extra for garnish

1 cup sugar

3 large egg whites

1 tablespoon maple syrup (the darker the better; we prefer Grade B)

Zest of 1 small orange or 1 tangerine

½ cup maple sugar, for rolling

**1.** Preheat the oven to 350°F. Line two rimmed sheet pans with parchment paper.

**2.** In a food processor, pulse the hazelnuts until they form a coarse meal. The pieces should not be larger than about ⅛-inch in diameter. (See the grinding nuts process on page 11.)

**3.** Transfer the hazelnut meal to a large bowl. Add the sugar, egg whites, maple syrup and zest. Using a rubber spatula or your hands (if you choose this method, wet your hands first to prevent the dough from sticking to them), mix the ingredients together until well combined. Cover the dough with plastic wrap and let rest for 10 minutes at room temperature, or until the dough is slightly dry to the touch.

**4.** Using your hands or a small scoop, form the dough into 1½-inch (1½-ounce) balls.

**5.** Pour the maple sugar in a small bowl. Roll each dough ball in the maple sugar, coating it completely. Place on a rimmed sheet pan, and top each with half a hazelnut by pressing the nut into the dough.

**6.** Bake for 12 minutes, or until lightly golden. Let the cookies cool fully before serving.

## Get Creative

· This cookie is also great with toasted hazelnuts. Simply place nuts on a rimmed sheet pan and toast for 10 minutes in a 350°F oven. Let cool before using.

· Try using any favorite nut like pecans or walnuts.

· Roll cookies using any of your favorite sugars like confectioners' sugar, sanding sugar, or even cinnamon sugar (¼ cup sugar mixed with 1 tablespoon cinammon).

# CHOCOLATE TRUFFLE COOKIES

*Yield: approximately 12 cookies*

¼ cup gluten-free flour mix (see inset)

¼ teaspoon salt

¼ teaspoon baking powder

2 tablespoons (1 ounce) unsalted butter

1½ cups (8 ounces) chopped dark chocolate*

½ cup sugar

2 large eggs, at room temperature

1½ teaspoons vanilla extract

Maldon sea salt, for garnish

*We prefer chocolate with 65–75 percent cocoa content for these cookies.*

1. Preheat the oven to 350°F. Line a rimmed sheet pan with parchment paper.

2. In a small bowl, whisk the gluten-free flour mix, salt and baking powder together. Set aside.

3. Cube the butter, and place it and the chocolate in a metal bowl. Place the bowl over a saucepan filled with 1 inch of water to create a double boiler. Melt the chocolate with the butter over medium-low heat, stirring often with a spatula, until completely smooth. Remove from the heat and let cool. (You can also melt the butter-chocolate mixture in a microwave-safe bowl by heating in a microwave oven for 20 seconds. After 20 seconds, stir and repeat until fully melted.)

4. In the bowl of a stand mixer fitted with a paddle attachment (or using a hand mixer), beat the sugar, eggs and vanilla extract on medium-high speed until the mixture is smooth and light in color, and the sugar looks mostly dissolved, about 2 minutes.

5. With the mixer on low, add the chocolate mixture to the egg mixture. Increase the speed to medium-high and beat for 30 seconds. Scrape down the sides of the bowl with a rubber spatula.

6. With the mixer off, add the gluten-free flour mixture to the bowl. Mix on medium-low speed for 20 seconds, scrape down the sides of the bowl, and then mix on medium-low for another 10 seconds. The dough will be gooey.

7. Using a scoop or a heaping tablespoon, form the dough into 1¼–1½-inch mounds (about 1½ ounces) and arrange them on the rimmed sheet pan.

8. Sprinkle the dough balls with Maldon sea salt, and bake for 8 to 10 minutes, turning the sheet halfway through baking. The top of the cookies should look cracked and just set when done. Let them cool fully before serving.

> ## GLUTEN-FREE FLOUR MIX
>
> 2 cups brown rice flour
> ⅔ cup potato starch
> ⅓ cup tapioca flour
>
> 1. Add all ingredients to a large bowl.
>
> 2. Whisk thoroughly until fully blended.

# BUTTERY SHORTBREAD

*Yield: 12 squares*

*When Agatha and I started to work on a shortbread base, we added as much butter to our recipe as possible, until the dough couldn't take any more. Incredibly tender and only a touch sweet, this shortbread lasts for up to 1 month in an airtight container.*

Softened butter,
for greasing the baking pan

2 cups all-purpose flour

1 teaspoon salt

1¼ cups (10 ounces) unsalted butter, cubed and cold

½ cup sugar

**1.** Preheat the oven to 275°F. Butter an 8 x 8-inch baking pan.

**2.** In a small bowl, whisk together the flour and salt. Set aside.

**3.** In the bowl of a stand mixer fitted with a paddle attachment (or using a hand mixer), cream together the cold butter and sugar on medium speed until light and barely fluffy, about 2 minutes. Do not overwhip the butter. It should be medium yellow in color and slightly cold to the touch.

**4.** Turn the mixer off. Add the flour mixture and mix on the lowest setting until just incorporated.

**5.** Remove the dough from the bowl, and press it into the prepared baking pan. We like to lay a sheet of plastic wrap over the dough and roll a small glass or bottle over it to ensure that it is rolled out evenly in the baking pan.

**6.** Bake for 40 to 45 minutes, or until lightly browned.

**7.** Cool the shortbread completely, and then score it and cut it into 2 x 2-inch squares. Use a spatula to remove them from the pan.

## Get Creative

Using the shortbread base, take the cookie to new levels with these following additions as inspiration for your own unique flavor profiles.

- Smoky Black Caraway–Dark Chocolate—Add 1½ tablespoons black caraway seeds (also called nigella) and ¼ cup chopped dark chocolate to the flour mixture. Before baking, sprinkle the dough with a light dusting of hickory-smoked sea salt (about ¼ teaspoon).

- Lemon–Pink Peppercorn—Add the zest of 1 lemon to the flour mixture. Before baking, sprinkle the pan evenly with about ½ teaspoon crushed pink peppercorns.

- Lavender-Vanilla—Add 1 teaspoon dried lavender to the flour mixture, and beat 1 teaspoon vanilla extract into the butter-sugar mixture.

- Toasted Pine Nut–Milk Chocolate—Toast 3 tablespoons pine nuts on a rimmed sheet pan in a 350°F oven for 10 minutes, or until lightly golden and fragrant. Let cool. Add the nuts, ¼ cup chopped milk chocolate and ½ teaspoon ground cinnamon to the flour mixture.

# THE STUMPTOWN SHORTY

*Yield: 24 cookies*

*This is our espresso–burnt sugar shortbread. Tender and buttery, it's the perfect cookie for coffee lovers.*

½ cup burnt sugar bits
(see recipe on page 92)

Softened butter, for greasing the
rimmed sheet pan + 1½ cups (24
tablespoons, 12 ounces) unsalted
butter, at room temperature

1 cup + 2 tablespoons
confectioners' sugar

1 teaspoon salt

2 tablespoons cold-brew coffee
(or fresh strong espresso, cooled)*

2¾ cups all-purpose flour

2 tablespoons very finely
ground espresso*

Turbinado sugar, for garnish

*\*We use Stumptown's Hair Bender
Espresso and the company's
cold brew for this recipe, but
any good-quality, finely ground
espresso and cold brew will do.*

**1.** Prepare the burnt sugar.

**2.** Heavily butter the bottom and sides of a 9 x 13-inch rimmed sheet pan.

**3.** In the bowl of a stand mixer fitted with a paddle attachment (or using a hand mixer), mix the 1½ cups butter, confectioners' sugar and salt together on low speed for 10 seconds, and then increase to medium-high speed and blend until light and fluffy, about 3 minutes. You want the butter mixture to be cold to the touch but not clumpy. Add the cold brew coffee at a low speed. Increase the speed to medium-high and mix until fully incorporated, about 30 seconds. Scrape down the sides of the bowl with a rubber spatula.

**4.** In a separate large bowl, whisk together the flour and ground espresso.

**5.** In a small bowl, mix ¼ cup of the flour mixture with the burnt sugar bits.

**6.** With the machine off, add half of the flour mixture to the butter mixture. Turn on low and mix about 30 seconds. Turn the machine off again, add the remaining half of the flour mixture and mix until just incorporated, another 30 seconds. Add the coated burnt sugar bits and mix on low speed for another 5 seconds, or until incorporated.

**7.** Press the dough evenly onto the prepared sheet pan. Place a layer of plastic wrap on top, and using a rolling pin, roll the dough to smooth the top and to ensure the dough is spread evenly on the rimmed sheet pan.

**8.** Preheat the oven to 350°F. Top the dough with turbinado sugar and place in the oven. Bake, turning halfway through, for 18 to 20 minutes, or until the dough looks puffy and the middle is set. Let the shortbread cool completely before cutting it into 24 approximately 2-inch squares.

# BURNT SUGAR

1 cup sugar

**1.** Spray a 9 x 13-inch rimmed sheet pan with nonstick cooking spray.

**2.** Pour the sugar into a heavy-bottomed skillet, and heat over medium-high heat. Mix the sugar continuously with a wooden spoon until it has completely melted (no visible granules) and is dark golden-brown. Do not burn the sugar. As you are stirring, break any sugar clumps apart with the wooden spoon. The entire process should take about 5 minutes.

**3.** Carefully pour the melted sugar onto the prepared rimmed sheet pan and, using a rubber spatula, spread it out evenly.

**4.** Let the burnt sugar cool completely at room temperature. Once it has completely hardened, about 30 minutes, turn the hardened sugar out onto a cutting board. Using a knife, chisel or small hammer, crack the sugar into bits about ¼-inch in size.

**5.** The burnt sugar bits can be kept indefinitely in an airtight container stored in a cool, dry place.

### Perfect Shortbread Squares

After rolling dough into a prepared rimmed sheet pan, place it into the refrigerator for a minimum of 4 hours, or until the dough is very firm. Line a 13 x 18-inch rimmed sheet pan (half-sheet pan) with parchment paper.

Remove the dough from the refrigerator. Using a ruler, mark the dough every 2¼ inches on each short side (9-inch side) of the rimmed sheet pan. On the 13-inch sides, mark the dough every 2⅙ inches. Using your ruler and a sharp knife, make a scored grid by connecting the marks in the dough. Cut along the lines with your knife. With a small offset spatula, remove the dough squares from the rimmed sheet pan and place them on the prepared rimmed sheet pan. Place the rimmed sheet pan in the freezer, and freeze for at least 15 minutes.

Preheat the oven to 350°F. Remove the dough squares from the freezer, sprinkle with turbinado sugar and bake for 18 to 20 minutes, turning halfway through. The cookies will be lightly golden when finished.

# PIES & TARTS

*Agatha* ❖ When Erin and I first discussed starting a food company, the one thing we were sure of was the name: Ovenly. We didn't know what type of business it would be or exactly what food we would offer. We considered all sorts of specialties—bar snacks, cookies, hand pies. The list was endless. We had both spent years accumulating a massive compilation of recipes, so we started by baking everything we knew how to bake, and then we kept narrowing down our ideas from there. It was a gargantuan undertaking. We sought advice from all sorts of friends, acquaintances and experts. Several people told us, "Never say 'no' in the beginning stages of business." We were determined to kick ass…so we said yes to everything. That was a big, fat mistake.

We baked. We catered. We consulted on menus. You name it, we did it. We spread ourselves thin, and instead of actually figuring out a business plan, we got lost in everything we were doing. In hindsight, we probably should have said "no" more often, but all that hustle also gave us the experiences we needed to finally settle on a game plan.

With our first few clients, we offered only "baker's choice." Basically, the client had to take whatever Erin and I made. This allowed us to perfect recipes that we had been working on for years, as well as try out new ones. It was a baker's dream come true. We were probably a bit overzealous with our flavor combinations. Matcha- mochi-hibiscus tea cakes come to mind. And sometimes we bit off more than we could chew and tried tackling overelaborate recipes, like cheesecake made with homemade ricotta, candied orange peels, homemade orange marmalade and freshly baked graham cracker crust. There were a lot of flops, but also a ton of crowd-pleasers. After a lot of trial and error, our menu *finally* came together.

One item that became popular (and later turned out to be a short-lived tease) was our Hot Tarts, a mature version of the Pop-Tart. Sour cherry and toasted almond (page 116), Nutella and banana with honey, peanut butter and Concord grape jam, sausage with scrambled eggs and sharp cheddar (page 114), and our ultimate favorite, salted caramel with crispy bacon (page 113)—all encased in a buttery, portable toasted pie crust. The Hot Tart was the ultimate breakfast fantasy.

Let me fill you in on a little secret: one of our first business ideas was for Ovenly to be a Hot Tart–only company. That idea lasted for about two weeks, but we did develop some killer recipes in the process, which was how they ended up on our menu months later. We became attached to our little Hot Tarts. But with only the two of us working at that point, they were too labor-intensive to justify including them on our regular menu. Plus, while Hot Tarts taste great at room temperature, they're better served warm, when the filling is slightly oozy and the pastry crust is toasty. Most coffee shops don't have ovens, so we apprehensively nixed the Hot Tarts and removed them from our menu. To this day, we still have fans (like Erin's brother Dan) requesting that we bring them back.

Along with the Hot Tarts, which we so briefly hawked, Erin and I share a serious affection for the variety of pies that we have offered. Double-crust pies, latticed pies, free-form pies, classic tarts—they all make us swoon. Like Hot Tarts, pies embody the subtle joys of homemade imperfection. And, yes, after a long day of pie making, when there's extra dough lying around, we still whip up the occasional batch of Hot Tarts. Putting them together actually requires very little forethought. All you need is a little spontaneity and a healthy appetite to make these comforting pockets of goodness at home. Just make sure you try them warm.

# PÂTE BRISÉE (FLAKY PIE CRUST)

*Yield: two 9-inch pie crusts*

*The mother of all pâte brisée (a fancy French word for "shortcrust pastry") recipes, we make this in large batches so that we have preportioned crusts on hand at all times—a trick to making pies, quiches and Hot Tarts in a pinch. The recipe can be adjusted for savory pies, and you can experiment with adding whole-wheat flour for nuttiness. Compared to the store-bought version, the flaky texture and buttery goodness of homemade pie crust is unrivaled. You can easily cut the pâte brisée recipes in half if you need only one crust!*

1 cup unsalted butter

2½ cups all-purpose flour

2 tablespoons sugar

1 teaspoon salt

¼ cup ice water

**1.** Cut butter into 1-inch cubes, and place in the freezer for 20 minutes, or until very cold.

**2.** In a food processor, add the flour, sugar and salt and process until combined. Add the butter and process until the mixture resembles coarse meal, about 15 seconds. (See process for making Pâte Brisée by hand on page 100.)

**3.** Pour in the ice water through the feed tube in a slow, steady stream, and process until the dough just holds together when pinched. If necessary, add more water. Do not process more than 30 seconds.

**4.** Turn the dough out onto a floured work surface and gather it into a ball. Divide the dough in half, flatten each half into a 6-inch disk, cover with plastic wrap and refrigerate for at least 1 hour and up to overnight before using. If not using right away, you can freeze unrolled dough for up to 1 month. Just let it thaw in the refrigerator overnight.

## Get Creative

### Pâte Brisée with Whole-Wheat Flour

· 1¾ cups all-purpose flour

· ¾ cup whole-wheat flour

· 2 tablespoons demerara sugar

· 1 teaspoon salt

· 1 cup unsalted butter, chilled and cut into 1-inch cubes

· ¼ cup + 3 tablespoons ice water

### Pâte Brisée for Savory Pies & Quiches

· 2½ cups all-purpose flour

· 1½ teaspoons sugar

· 1 teaspoon salt

· 1 cup unsalted butter, chilled and cut into 1-inch cubes

· ¼ cup + 3 tablespoons ice water

**5.** After the dough has chilled sufficiently, remove 1 disk from the refrigerator and place it on a lightly floured surface. Roll the dough into a 12-inch circle. To prevent the dough from sticking to your surface and to ensure uniform thickness, keep lifting it up and turning it a quarter turn as you roll. Always roll from the center of the dough outward.

**6.** Fold the dough in half and gently transfer it to a 9-inch pie pan. Press the dough gently against the sides of the pan. Brush off any excess flour and tuck the overhanging dough under itself, crimping as desired. Cover with plastic wrap and refrigerate for about 30 minutes before filling.

**7.** If you are making a crust to top your pie, remove the second disk of dough from the refrigerator and roll it into a 12-inch circle on a lightly floured surface. You can choose how to top the pie with the crust.

- Cover the pie completely with the top crust, pinch the edges of the bottom and top crusts together, and cut 3 to 4 thin steam vents in the center (see the double crust process on pages 104–105).
- Make a lattice top (see lattice process on pages 108–109).
- With a cookie cutter, cut out about 20 shapes. Place the shapes on a parchment–lined rimmed sheet pan, cover with plastic wrap and place in the refrigerator for about 30 minutes before using.

**8.** Once you fill the pie, cover it with the top crust, using the method of choice, and bake according to recipe instructions.*

*If you have to blind bake your pie crust for an open-faced pie or tart, or for a pie that has a separately prepared filling, lay a piece of parchment twice the width of the pie pan over the crust and then fill the paper with pie weights or dry beans. For a par-baked crust, bake at 425°F for 10 to 15 minutes, or until the edges are barely golden. For a fully baked crust, bake at 425°F for 20 to 25 minutes until the edges are barely golden. Carefully remove the parchment and weights, reduce the heat to 375°F and continue to bake for 5 to 10 minutes more, or until the crust is evenly golden.*

*We recommend finishing a filled pie directly on the bottom of the oven floor, or on a pizza stone. It will help the bottom crust to crisp.*

## MAKING PIE DOUGH AND PÂTE BRISÉE BY HAND

Be sure to chill your pâte brisée and other to-be-rolled doughs (unless otherwise noted) as indicated in the recipes. Refrigerating helps the gluten to relax and makes the dough more elastic. Freezing rolled doughs helps them to retain their shape during baking, which will result in more perfect-looking and beautiful desserts.

Flatten your dough into a 6-inch disk (or into a 9 x 15-inch rectangle in the case of the Hot Tarts) before chilling. This will make it easier to roll the dough into the proper shape later on.

01  In a large bowl, whisk together the flour, sugar and salt, and then add the butter. Rub the butter and flour together until the mixture has a cornmeal-like consistency and no large butter clumps remain.

02  Add the ice water in a slow stream, and mix with a spoon. If the dough is difficult to mix with a spoon, use your hands.

03  Press the dough together to loosely combine any ragged pieces of dough.

04  Turn the dough out onto a floured work surface, and with the heel of your hand, press the dough together, using an outward rubbing motion. This is to incorporate all the butter into the dough.

05  Halve the dough, and form each half into a ball.

06  Press and shape each half into a 6-inch-wide disk (about an inch high) before refrigerating.

01

02

03

04

*It is important to start with cold ingredients. We like to freeze everything (even the flour) for 20 minutes before preparing the pâte brisée.*

# BLUE CHEESE APPLE PIE WITH TOASTED WALNUTS

*Yield: one 9-inch pie*

*Originally, we were going to make a classic apple-walnut pie for the shop, but that sounded too simple. We rummaged through the fridge and found some Bayley Hazen Blue Cheese from Jasper Hill Farm. We tossed the pungent but sweet cheese onto the chunky apple filling, added freshly cracked black pepper and popped the pie in the oven. The result was juicy, sweet and subtly sharp, and impressed both our cheese- and pie-loving friends alike. It is a great option for the fall season and is best served with a jug of red wine or a digestif.*

Pâte Brisée
(see recipe on page 98)

¾ cup coarsely chopped walnuts

2 pounds (approximately 5 to 6 medium) apples (a mix of Winesap, Jonagold or Golden Delicious works best)

¼ cup lemon juice (about 1 lemon)

½ cup sugar + 1 tablespoon, for garnish

¼ cup (packed) light brown sugar

¼ cup all-purpose flour

1 tablespoon cornstarch

1 teaspoon ground cinnamon

½ teaspoon salt

¼ teaspoon ground nutmeg

¼ teaspoon freshly cracked black pepper

⅓ cup + 2 tablespoons crumbled mild, dry blue cheese

1 tablespoon unsalted butter

1 large egg yolk, for brushing

1 tablespoon heavy cream (or whole milk), for brushing

**1.** Prepare the Pâte Brisée recipe (2 crusts). Remove 1 disk of the pâte brisée from the refrigerator 10 minutes before rolling. Roll out the disk to line the bottom of a 9-inch pie pan (the dough should be about 12 inches in diameter). Transfer dough and press into the pan, and then chill it in the refrigerator for at least 30 minutes, or freeze for 10 minutes (or up to overnight) before using. (See double crust process on pages 104–105.)

**2.** Preheat the oven to 350°F. Toast the walnuts on a rimmed sheet pan for 10 minutes, or until golden and fragrant. Remove the walnuts from the oven and let cool.

**3.** While the walnuts toast, peel, core and cut the apples into ⅛- to ¼-inch-thick slices, and place in a large bowl. Add the lemon juice and then toss. Set aside.

**4.** In a small bowl, whisk together the sugars, flour, cornstarch, cinnamon, salt, nutmeg and pepper until well combined. Add the flour-sugar mixture to the apples. Mix with a rubber spatula or a wooden spoon until the apples are uniformly coated. Then mix in the toasted walnuts.

**5.** Fill the prepared bottom pie crust with the apple mixture, and then top with the blue cheese crumbles. Dot the top of the filling with the 1 tablespoon butter. Place the pie in the refrigerator while rolling out second disk of pâte brisée.

**6.** Roll out the second disk of the pâte brisée to 12 inches in diameter. Remove the pie from the refrigerator, and top with the second pâte brisée crust, covering the pie completely. Tuck the edges under the bottom pie crust, and then pinch the edges of the bottom and top crusts together (you can also press the edges together with a fork). Cut 3 to 4 steam vents in the center of the top crust. (See double crust process on pages 104–105.)

**7.** Refrigerate the pie for 1 hour or freeze for 30 minutes before baking.

**8.** When the pie has about 15 minutes left to chill, position the oven rack in the bottom third of the oven, and then preheat the oven to 425°F.

**9.** Prepare an egg wash by whisking together the egg yolk and the cream.

**10.** Remove the pie from the refrigerator or freezer. Using a pastry brush, brush the top of the pie crust evenly with the egg wash, and sprinkle with the remaining 1 tablespoon sugar.

**11.** Place the pie on a rimmed sheet pan. Bake it for 15 minutes, or until the crust just begins to turn golden. Reduce the heat to 350°F, and bake 40 to 45 minutes more, turning halfway through baking, or until the crust is golden and the juices are bubbling through the steam vents. Keep an eye on the pie. If the edges of the crust brown too quickly, cover it loosely with aluminum foil.

**12.** Transfer the pie to a wire rack and let cool for at least 1 hour before serving.

# DOUBLE CRUST PROCESS

01  After rolling out the dough to a 12-inch circle (⅛- to ¼-inch thick), use a bench scraper and fold the dough into quarters. Gently transfer the dough to a pie plate and unfold.

02  Lightly press the dough against the sides and bottom of the pie plate.

03  Use scissors to trim the overhang on the edges to a ½-inch overhang.

04  Pour your prepared filling into the prepared pie plate.

If using a fruit filling such as apple, mound the filling into the crust. Place in refrigerator while rolling out top crust into another 12-inch round.

05  Repeat step one, and fold dough into quarters. Unfold dough over filling, and again trim edges to ½-inch overhang as in step 3.

06  Fold the edges of the top crust under the edges of the bottom crust. Press the two together to form a seal.

07  Flute the edges by pinching the dough into ridges between the index finger of one hand and the thumb and index finger of the other hand. Place in freezer for 30 minutes before baking.

08  Cut 3 to 4 thin steam vents into the top crust with a paring knife, brush with egg wash and sprinkle with sugar before baking.

# PEAR, SOUR CHERRY & CARDAMOM PIE

*Yield: one 9-inch pie*

*Sour cherry season in New York is fleeting. We bake this pie a lot, but to do so, we have to stockpile our sour cherries in the summer and freeze what we can so that we are well prepared for the arrival of pear season in the fall. The vibrant colors and warm spice make it an ideal autumnal pie.*

Pâte Brisée
(see recipe on page 98)

2 pounds (about 5 medium) firm, ripe pears (we like to use a mix of D'Anjou and Bosc)

1½ cups fresh sour cherries*

¼ cup (packed) light brown sugar

¼ cup (packed) dark brown sugar

¼ cup all-purpose flour

1¼ teaspoons ground cardamom (preferably freshly ground)

½ teaspoon ground cinnamon

½ teaspoon salt

1 tablespoon fresh lemon juice

1 teaspoon vanilla extract

1 tablespoon unsalted butter

1 large egg yolk, for brushing

1 tablespoon heavy cream, for brushing

1 tablespoon sugar, for garnish

*\* If unavailable, use frozen.*

**1.** Prepare the Pâte Brisée recipe (2 crusts). Remove 1 disk of the pâte brisée from the refrigerator 10 minutes before rolling. Roll out the disk to line the bottom of a 9-inch pie pan (the dough should be about 12 inches in diameter). Press the dough into the pan, and then chill it in the refrigerator for at least 30 minutes, or freeze for 10 minutes (or up to overnight) before using. (See Double Crust Process steps 1 to 4 on pages 104–105.)

**2.** Peel, core and cut the pears into about ⅛-inch-thick slices, and place in a large bowl. Remove the pits from the sour cherries, using your hands or a cherry pitter. Halve the cherries and add them to the pears. Set aside.

**3.** In a small bowl, whisk together the sugars, flour, cardamom, cinnamon and salt until well combined. Add the flour-sugar mixture to the pears and cherries, mix until just combined, and then add the lemon juice and vanilla extract. Mix until the fruit is uniformly coated.

**4.** Fill the prepared bottom pie crust with the pear-cherry filling, mounding the fruit in the center of the pan. Dot the top of the filling with the 1 tablespoon butter. Place the pie in the refrigerator while rolling out second disk of pâte brisée.

**5.** Roll out the second disk of the pâte brisée to 12 inches in diameter. Remove the pie from the refrigerator, and top with the second pâte brisée crust, covering the pie completely or make a lattice top (see Lattice Process on pages 108–109). Tuck the edges under the bottom pie crust, and then pinch the edges of the bottom and top crusts together (you can also press the edges together with a fork). Cut 3 to 4 steam vents in the center of the top crust.

**6.** Refrigerate the pie for 1 hour or freeze for 30 minutes before baking.

**7.** When the pie has about 15 minutes left to chill, position the oven rack in the bottom third of the oven, and then preheat the oven to 425°F.

**8.** Prepare an egg wash by whisking together the egg yolk and cream.

**9.** Remove the pie from the refrigerator or freezer. Using a pastry brush, brush the top of the pie crust evenly with the egg wash, and sprinkle with the sugar.

**10.** Place the pie on a rimmed sheet pan. Bake it for 15 minutes, or until the crust just begins to turn golden. Reduce the heat to 350°F, and bake 40 to 45 minutes more, turning halfway through baking, or until the crust is golden and the juices are bubbling through the steam vents. Keep an eye on the pie. If the edges of the crust brown too quickly, cover it loosely with aluminum foil.

**11.** Transfer the pie to a wire rack and let cool for at least 1 hour before serving.

# LATTICE PROCESS

01 Follow Double Crust Process steps 1 to 4 (see page 104). Roll out top crust to a 12-inch round (⅛ to ¼-inch thick). Using a knife or a pizza cutter, trim the edges off of the sides to square them.

02 Using a ruler, cut the dough into 6, approximately 2-inch strips (you can do more—8 or 10 or 12—here, just ensure each strip is of equal width). The bigger the lattice pieces, the easier it will be to weave them together. Transfer to a parchment-lined rimmed sheet pan and refrigerate for 30 minutes.

03 To weave the lattice, lay one strip vertically across the left-side of the pie (as it is oriented toward your body). Lay another strip over that strip at the bottom of the pie. Lay a third strip parallel to the first strip and OVER the second strip. Lay a fourth strip parallel to the third strip, and under the second strip (pick up the second strip and place the fourth strip under it).

04 Lay a fifth strip parallel to the second strip. Pick up the first strip and place it over the fifth strip. Place the fifth strip over the third strip, and then under the fourth strip.

05 Lay the final strip over the first strip, weave it under the third strip, and then over the fourth strip.

06 Trim the strip to a ½-inch overhang.

07 Fold the lattice under the edges of the bottom crust. Press the two together to form a seal.

08 Follow step 7 of the Double Crust Process on page 104 for fluting edges of the pie, or press together with a fork. Place in freezer for thirty minutes before baking.

09 Brush with egg wash, sprinkle with one tablespoon sugar and bake until golden and juices are bubbling.

01

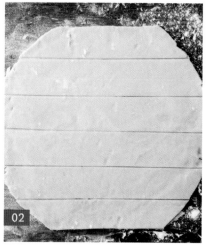
02

03

# NECTARINE, BLUEBERRY & VANILLA BEAN RUSTIC TART

*Yield: one approximately 10-inch tart*

*We're obsessive about consistency in our baked goods, especially when it comes to appearance. With pies, it's a different story. There's something inherently charming about pies that don't look perfect. We prefer our pies to be handmade and rustic—like this free-form tart. Use whatever fruit you have available, and don't be afraid to improvise or to be spontaneous.*

Pâte Brisée with Whole-Wheat Flour (see recipe on page 98)

2 large, ripe nectarines (about 2½ cups sliced)

½ cup fresh blueberries

1 vanilla bean

¼ cup all-purpose flour

¼ cup (packed) light brown sugar

2 teaspoons + 1 tablespoon sugar

1 tablespoon unsalted butter

1 large egg yolk, for brushing

1 tablespoon water, for brushing

**1.** Prepare the Pâte Brisée with Whole-Wheat Flour recipe (you will need only 1 crust, either halve the brisée recipe or save the second crust for later use). Remove 1 disk of the pâte brisée from the refrigerator 10 minutes before rolling.

**2.** Preheat the oven to 425°F. Line a rimmed sheet pan with parchment paper.

**3.** Remove the pits from the nectarines and cut the halves into about ¼-inch-thick slices. Add them to a large bowl along with the blueberries. Scrape the seeds from the vanilla bean, and mix them into the fruit with a wooden spoon or a rubber spatula.

**4.** In a small bowl, mix the flour, brown sugar and 2 teaspoons of the sugar together. Add this to the fruit mixture, and mix until the fruit is uniformly coated.

**5.** On a lightly floured, clean surface, roll the disk of pâte brisée into an approximately 12-inch circle. Fold the dough in half and gently transfer it to the prepared rimmed sheet pan.

**6.** Mound the fruit in the center of the dough, in about a 7-inch circle. Dot it with the butter. Fold the outer edges of the dough over the filling all the way around the tart in an accordion pattern. The crust will overlap on itself. The crust should not cover the filling completely, and will leave about a 3½- to 4-inch opening in the center of the tart.

**7.** Prepare an egg wash by whisking together the egg yolk and water. Using a pastry brush, brush the top of the crust evenly with the egg wash and sprinkle with the remaining 1 tablespoon sugar.

**8.** Bake for 30 to 40 minutes, or until the crust is golden brown. Let the tart cool for 15 to 20 minutes before slicing and serving.

# CARAMEL BACON HOT TARTS

*Yield: 4 Hot Tarts*

*These Hot Tarts are our mature version of Pop-Tarts. The salty-smooth caramel is followed by a smoky, crispy bacon crunch. A dose of sweet-savory decadence.*

Pâte Brisée
(see recipe on page 98)

2 slices bacon

1 tablespoon + 1 teaspoon
light brown sugar

¼ cup + 2 tablespoons
chilled Salted Caramel Sauce
(see recipe on page 190)

1 large egg yolk, for brushing

1 tablespoon water, for brushing

**1.** Cook the bacon in a skillet until crisp and done. Transfer the bacon to a paper towel–lined plate to drain off any excess grease. Let cool.

**2.** Prepare the Pâte Brisée recipe (you will need only 1 crust, either halve the brisée recipe or save the second crust for later use). Remove 1 disk of the pâte brisée from the refrigerator 10 minutes before rolling.

**3.** On a lightly floured, clean surface, roll the disk of pâte brisée into an approximate 9 x 15-inch rectangle. (See Hot Tart Process on pages 114–115.) To prevent the dough from sticking to the counter and to ensure a uniform thickness, keep lifting and turning the pâte brisée a quarter turn as you roll.

**4.** Using a ruler, measure the dough and mark a rectangle that is *exactly* 9 x 15 inches. Then cut the ragged edges off, leaving straight edges, with a knife or pizza cutter. Cut the dough lengthwise every 3¾ inches. This will result in four 3¾ x 9-inch rectangles.

**5.** Layer ½ strip of bacon on the bottom half of 1 rectangle and then sprinkle 1 teaspoon of the light brown sugar over the bacon. Top with 1½ tablespoons of the chilled Salted Caramel Sauce. Repeat these steps for the remaining 3 rectangles.

**6.** Using a pastry brush or your finger, brush water on the outer edges of the top half of each rectangle to help seal the edges. Then fold in half, and press the edges together with your fingers to seal.

**7.** Crimp the edges together with a fork to seal more. With your knife or pizza cutter, remove the ragged edges by cutting the Hot Tarts into perfect 3¾ x 4½-inch rectangles. Using a fork, gently poke a few holes in the top of each Hot Tart.

**8.** Transfer Hot Tarts to a rimmed sheet pan lined with parchment paper. Freeze the Hot Tarts for 10 minutes.

**9.** Preheat the oven to 400°F. Prepare an egg wash by whisking the egg yolk with the water in a small bowl until smooth.

**10.** Remove the Hot Tarts from the freezer. Brush them with the egg wash, and bake for 20 to 22 minutes, or until just golden. Let the tarts cool before serving.

### More Hot Tart Fillings Ideas

- Nutella, Banana & Honey—For 1 Hot Tart, layer 1½ tablespoons of Nutella with 4 slices of banana and drizzle with 1 teaspoon of honey.

- Peanut Butter & Concord Grape Jam—For 1 Hot Tart, layer 1½ tablespoons of peanut butter (or another nut butter), followed by 2 teaspoons of Concord grape (or another fruit) jam.

- Sausage with Scrambled Egg & Sharp Cheddar—For 4 Hot Tarts, scramble 2 eggs and cook 1 large (or 2 small) breakfast sausages. Divide the eggs evenly among the 4 tarts. Slice the sausage for each tart and layer over the egg on each tart. Top with 1 table-spoon shredded sharp cheddar.

## HOT TART PROCESS

01 Roll out the dough, and then use a ruler to measure *exactly* 9-inches in height x 15-inches in width. Cut off the ragged edges of the dough with a knife, and then cut the dough lengthwise every 3¾ inches.

02 Layer the bacon on the bottom half of each rectangle.

03 Sprinkle with light brown sugar and top with Salted Caramel Sauce.

04 Brush water on the outer edges of the top half of each rectangle.

05 Fold the top half of each rectangle over the bottom half.

06 Press the edges together with your fingers to seal.

07 Crimp the edges with a fork.

08 Trim off the ragged edges with a knife, cutting each Hot Tart into a 3¾ x 4½-inch rectangle.

09 Using a fork, gently poke a few holes in the top of each Hot Tart.

01

02

03

# CHERRY ALMOND HOT TARTS WITH LEMON GLAZE

*Yield: 4 Hot Tarts*

*We like to eat these for breakfast. The toasted almonds pack in a lot of protein (kind of healthy, right?) and cut the tartness of the cherries and lemon, rounding out the flavor for a well-balanced, yet slightly sweet treat.*

Pâte Brisée
(see recipe on page 98)

**CHERRY ALMOND FILLING**

⅓ cup raw almonds

½ cup water

1 cup dried cherries

Juice of half a small lemon

**EGG WASH**

1 large egg yolk

1 tablespoon water

**LEMON GLAZE**

¼ cup confectioners' sugar

2½ teaspoons lemon juice
(preferably fresh)

**1.** Preheat the oven to 350°F.

**2.** Prepare the Pâte Brisée recipe (you will need only 1 crust, either halve the brisée recipe or save the second crust for later use). Remove 1 disk of the pâte brisée from the refrigerator 10 minutes before rolling.

**3.** Toast the almonds on a rimmed sheet pan in a preheated 350°F oven for 10 minutes, or until fragrant. Let cool 5 minutes. In a food processor, grind the toasted almonds into a fine meal. Increase the oven to 400°F.

**4.** Boil the water. Place the cherries in a small bowl and pour the boiling water over them. Soak for 10 minutes, and then use a fine-mesh sieve to drain the water from the cherries into a separate bowl, reserving the water.

**5.** Add the cherries to the bowl of the food processor with the finely ground almonds. Add the lemon juice and 3 tablespoons of the reserved water. Pulse in 15-second intervals for a total of 1 minute, or until a thick, pasty jam forms. Scrape down the sides of the bowl after each pulse. The cherry mixture should be thick but spreadable. If it is too thick, add another tablespoon of the reserved water and pulse to combine.

**6.** On a lightly floured, clean surface, roll the disk of pâte brisée into an approximate 9 x 15-inch rectangle (see Hot Tart Process on pages 114–115). To prevent the dough from sticking to the counter and to ensure a uniform thickness, keep lifting and turning the pâte brisée a quarter turn as you roll.

**7.** Using a ruler, measure the dough and mark a rectangle that is *exactly* 9 x 15 inches. Then cut the ragged edges off, leaving straight edges, with a knife or pizza cutter. Cut the dough lengthwise every 3¾ inches. This will result in four 3¾ x 9-inch rectangles.

**8.** Spread 2 tablespoons of the cherry-almond mixture evenly on the bottom half of 1 rectangle, leaving about 1-inch around the bottom and side edges. Repeat for the remaining 3 rectangles.

**9.** Using a pastry brush or your finger, brush water on the outer edges of the top half of each rectangle to help seal the edges. Then fold in half, and press the edges together with your fingers to seal.

**10.** Crimp the edges together with a fork to seal fully. With your knife or pizza cutter, remove the ragged edges by cutting the Hot Tarts into perfect 3¾ x 4½-inch rectangles. Using a fork, gently poke a few holes in the top of each Hot Tart. Freeze the Hot Tarts for 10 minutes.

**11.** Line a rimmed sheet pan with parchment paper. Prepare an egg wash by whisking the egg yolk with the water in a small bowl until smooth.

**12.** Remove the Hot Tarts from the freezer. Arrange on prepared sheet pan. Brush them with the egg wash, and bake for 20 to 22 minutes, or until just golden.

**13.** While the Hot Tarts are baking, prepare the lemon glaze by whisking together the confectioners' sugar and lemon juice until smooth. Drizzle the glaze over the baked Hot Tarts and let cool for 10 minutes. Serve warm!

# GOAT CHEESE, SPRING ONION & CHIVE QUICHE

*Yield: one 10-inch quiche*

*Quiche is versatile and almost effortless, and can be enjoyed for breakfast, lunch or dinner. We love using creamy goat cheese paired with onions and chives in ours, but quiche is also a great base for using up whatever produce and cheese you have lying around. Since eggs are the foundation of this recipe, be sure to use the freshest (preferably local) eggs you can find. This quiche can be served warm or at room temperature, and it can be prepared a day ahead and refrigerated overnight. If you chill it, let it sit for 30 minutes before serving.*

Pâte Brisée for Savory Pies & Quiches
(see recipe on page 98)

**FILLING**

6 large eggs

1 cup heavy cream

1 teaspoon salt

½ teaspoon black pepper

4 spring onions, root ends trimmed and chopped into ¼-inch dice

⅓ cup crumbled goat cheese

3 tablespoons finely minced chives

**1.** Prepare the Pâte Brisée for Savory Pies & Quiches recipe (you will need only 1 crust). Remove 1 disk of the pâte brisée from the refrigerator 10 minutes before rolling. Roll out the disk to about 12 inches in diameter to line the bottom of a 10-inch tart pan with a removable bottom. Fold the dough into quarters and gently transfer it to the tart pan. Gently fit the dough into the pan, and using your fingers, press it into the bottom of the pan and up the fluted sides. Be sure that the dough fits snugly where the bottom and the sides of the pan meet.

**2.** Trim any excess dough by gently running your rolling pin over the top of the pan, which will make the top of the dough even with the top of the pan and will cut off any excess. Chill in the refrigerator for at least 30 minutes or freeze for 10 minutes before using.

**3.** Preheat the oven to 375°F.

**4.** Remove the tart pan from the refrigerator, and line the crust with parchment paper at least 18 inches long. Fill the parchment paper with pie weights or dried beans, ensuring the weights fit snugly against the sides of the pan. Bake for 20 minutes. Remove the crust from the oven, and carefully lift the parchment paper with the weights inside of it out of the tart pan.

**5.** Place the tart pan back in the oven and bake for another 10 to 15 minutes, or until the crust just starts to brown. Set it aside to cool for about 10 minutes.

**6.** Reduce the oven temperature to 350°F.

**7.** While the crust is cooling, prepare the filling. In a medium bowl, whisk together the eggs, cream, salt and pepper.

**8.** Arrange the spring onions on the bottom of the cooled crust in an even layer. Place spoonfuls of goat cheese evenly over the onions, and then sprinkle the chives over the whole thing.

**9.** Place the tart pan on a rimmed sheet pan. Pour the egg filling into the crust.

**10.** Bake for 35 to 40 minutes, or until the edges are set and the quiche jiggles only slightly in the center. Let cool before serving.

**Seasonal and Gluten-Free Variations**

- Cheddar, Garlic Scape & Fresh Herb—Layer ¾ cup shredded sharp cheddar evenly over the bottom of the tart crust, followed by ¼ cup sliced garlic scapes and 2 teaspoons minced fresh thyme. Top with the egg mixture and bake.

- Zucchini, Shallot & Mint—Sauté 2 cups sliced zucchini, ¼ cup chopped shallots and 1 minced garlic clove in 1 tablespoon olive oil and let cool. Drain any excess liquid, and layer evenly over the bottom of the tart crust. Top with ¼ cup grated Parmesan and ¼ cup coarsely chopped mint leaves. Top with the egg mixture and bake.

- Bacon & Blue Cheese—Layer ⅓ to ½ cup crumbled blue cheese evenly over the bottom of the tart crust, followed by ⅓ cup chopped cooked bacon. Top with the egg mixture and bake.

- Gluten-Free—Omit the crust completely, and instead butter a tart pan with a non-removable bottom. Place the pan on a rimmed sheet pan. Pour the egg filling directly into the prepared pan, layer with filling of choice, and bake until the top is golden brown, 25 to 30 minutes.

# BROWNIES
# & BARS

*Erin* ❖ Since Agatha and I started out as home cooks, we never had a reason to bake more than a few dozen servings of any one recipe. But soon after we launched Ovenly, we began receiving orders for our brownies and bars in the *hundreds* of dozens. Making them without diminishing their quality, taste or appearance was a major challenge, and the learning curve was steep.

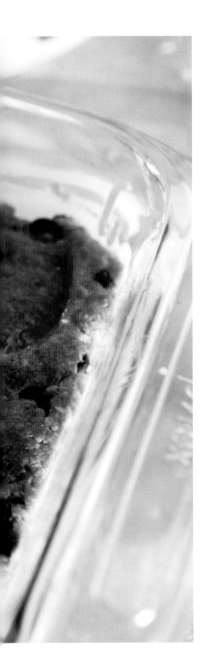

Agatha and I are anal about our baked goods. (Let's be honest. We're borderline obsessive-compulsive.) And anything that had to be sliced posed particularly difficult problems for us: How do we make a zillion bars and then cut them all perfectly *and* quickly? And how do we do that without spending a googolplex of dollars on expensive machinery? Broken edges and crooked lines were driving us batty and costing us money. Our freezer was bursting at the seams with abnormally shaped coconut blondies that we couldn't (and wouldn't) sell.

Then, through the grapevine, we heard of a mysterious crew of brainy twentysomethings who were launching a distillery and a custom machine shop in an even more uninhabited corner of Brooklyn than our own in Red Hook. We had to check it out, so Agatha and I hopped into Wedgie (our temperamental SUV) and drove south.

Industry City Distillery (ICD), and its parent company, The City Foundry, occupy an airy twelve-thousand-square-foot industrial loft overlooking the East River in a cavernous manufacturing district composed of blocks of identical, looming steel and concrete buildings. When Agatha and I walked into ICD, inventive-looking machines, including a laboratory built on steel stilts and a bioreactor nicknamed "Tom"—we're still not 100 percent sure what a bioreactor is—greeted us. An employee covered in greasy Carhartt work pants gave us a tour of the facilities, and when we arrived at the communal kitchen, we were shocked by its state. Marginally edible food and half-eaten bags of tortilla chips lined its makeshift shelves. In fact, the first time we visited, one staffer was eating a late breakfast that included something he called a "meat log."

First we thought, *Yuck*. And then, *Bingo!*

Agatha and I immediately knew our angle. If this ragtag group of engineers and artists could dream up a precise sizing and slicing tool for us, we would be able to pay them with something worth much more than money: abnormally shaped coconut blondies. We proposed the barter to the boys and shook hands in agreement. They developed an ingenious, simple frame and cutting tool welded out of used scrap metal for us (which we still use today). And we kept the boys fed.

Now, we don't suppose that our readers are going to take the time to come to Brooklyn to have custom cookware made for them, but you can take these ideas with you: you can use a file to mark your own rimmed sheet pans, and a dedicated heavy steel rod or yardstick can help you to make the cuts. Or you can just do what we do when we're baking at home, and cut your favorite bars into whatever sizes and shapes you like.

# CINNAMON & ANCHO CHILE BROWNIES

*Yield: one 8 x 8-inch pan, cut into 16 squares*

*While I was growing up, brownies were the staple dessert in my house. My mom made them from a mix and added chocolate chips. Then, when the brownies came out of the oven, she topped them with two or three Hershey's chocolate bars. When the bars melted, she spread the gooey chocolate in a thin layer over the baked batter. As it hardened, I would sneak a bite. There's nothing like a warm brownie with melty chocolate on top. My mom still makes her special brownies for me when I visit, and I still sneak an early taste. Try yours the same way—filled with chocolate chips and topped with your favorite chocolate.*

Softened unsalted butter and all-purpose flour, for preparing the baking pan

1 cup (6 ounces) chopped dark chocolate*

1 stick + 2 tablespoons (10 tablespoons, 5 ounces) unsalted butter, cubed

1 cup sugar

3 large eggs, at room temperature

⅓ cup (packed) light brown sugar

1 teaspoon vanilla extract

⅔ cup all-purpose flour

3 tablespoons American-process cocoa powder

1½ teaspoons ground cinnamon

¾ teaspoon ancho chile powder

¼ teaspoon salt

Confectioners' sugar, for dusting (optional)

*We prefer chocolate with 60 percent cocoa content or higher.*

**1.** Preheat the oven to 350°F. Grease an 8 x 8-inch baking pan with softened butter and dust the pan with flour.

**2.** Place the chocolate and butter in a medium metal bowl. Place the bowl over a saucepan filled with 1 inch of cold water to create a double boiler. Melt the chocolate and butter over medium-low heat, stirring often with a rubber spatula, until completely smooth. Remove from the heat and let cool. (You can also melt the mixture in a microwave-safe bowl by heating in a microwave oven for 20 seconds. After 20 seconds, stir and repeat until fully melted.)

**3.** In a separate medium bowl, whisk together sugar, eggs, light brown sugar and vanilla extract until smooth. Add the cooled chocolate mixture and combine.

**4.** In a small bowl, whisk together the flour, cocoa powder, cinnamon, chile powder and salt. Add the flour mixture to the chocolate-egg mixture, and combine with a spatula until smooth and uniform. Pour the batter into the prepared baking pan.

**5.** Bake for 30 minutes, or until the top looks crisp and cracks begin to form. If a toothpick does not come out perfectly clean when you test the brownies, that is okay. Better to have slightly underdone brownies than overdone ones. They will set as they cool.

**6.** Cool completely before cutting the brownies into 16, 2 x 2-inch squares. Serve plain or dusted with confectioners' sugar.

## Get Creative

- Remove the spices for a simple fudgy brownie.

- Fold in ½ cup of your favorite chopped nuts.

- Add ½ cup of your favorite chocolate chips.

- Add an additional ¾ cup chocolate chips to the top of the brownies as soon as they come out of the oven. Once the chocolate melts, spread it over the top with an offset spatula. Let it cool and harden before serving.

- Or do as my mom does and use a Hershey's chocolate bar for topping.

# SALTY SUPER DARK CHOCOLATE BROWNIES

*Yield: one 9 x 13-inch pan, cut into 15 bars*

*While we love the spice in our Cinnamon & Ancho Chile Brownies, we wanted something chewier, richer and more decadent. This dark chocolate brownie hits the nail on the head. We use a dark Dutch-process cocoa from Guittard (we recommend taking the time to order some [see Essential Tools & Ingredients on page 9]). Black in color and deeply bittersweet, both the color and the flavor will add a unique twist to any dessert that calls for cocoa powder.*

Softened unsalted butter and all-purpose flour, for preparing the baking pan

1 cup American-process cocoa powder

½ cup all-purpose flour

¼ cup dark Dutch-process cocoa powder (see Essential Tools & Ingredients on page 9)

2 teaspoons Turkish (very finely ground) espresso, or instant espresso*

¾ teaspoon salt

1 cup (8 ounces, 16 tablespoons) unsalted butter, cubed

4 large eggs, at room temperature

¾ cup sugar

¾ cup (packed) dark brown sugar

Maldon sea salt, for garnish

*We prefer Stumptown's Hair Bender Espresso*

**1.** Preheat the oven to 350°F. Grease a 9 x 13-inch baking pan with softened butter and dust the pan with flour.

**2.** In a medium bowl, sift together the American-process cocoa powder, flour, dark Dutch-process cocoa powder, espresso and salt. Set aside.

**3.** In a small saucepan over low heat (or in a small, microwave-safe bowl in a microwave oven), melt the butter and set aside to cool.

**4.** In another small bowl, whisk the eggs until the yolks are broken. Add the cooled butter and sugars, whisking until smooth.

**5.** Add the dry mixture to the wet mixture. Mix with a wooden spoon or a rubber spatula to combine completely.

**6.** Pour the batter into the prepared baking pan and sprinkle with the Maldon sea salt.

**7.** Bake for 35 minutes, or until the center is set and a toothpick inserted in the center of the brownies comes out clean.

**8.** Cool completely before cutting the bars into 15, approximately 3 x 2½-inch rectangles (or whatever size you prefer).

*Note*

*For thicker brownies, use an 8 x 8-inch pan, and bake for 45 minutes, or until a toothpick inserted in the center of the brownies comes out clean.*

# MONTEGO BAY BARS
## (Date Chocolate Jam Bars)

*Yield: one 13 x 9-inch pan, cut into 15 bars*

*A few years ago my mom, who loves dates, sent me a variation of this recipe. Agatha and I tinkered with it—adding black caraway and nutty spelt—to make it more Ovenly-ish. When we finished our experimenting, I called Mom to ask what was up with the "Montego Bay" in the title. She responded that dates seemed "kinda Caribbean." The name stuck.*

Softened unsalted butter, for greasing the baking pan

3 cups dried, pitted dates, chopped into ¼-inch disks

1½ cups water

3 ounces dark chocolate (65 to 75 percent cocoa content)

¼ cup sugar

1½ cups spelt flour

1½ cups rolled oats

½ cup coarsely chopped raw pecans, walnuts or hazelnuts

2 tablespoons (⅛ cup) black caraway seeds

1 teaspoon salt

½ teaspoon baking soda

10 tablespoons (5 ounces) unsalted butter, at room temperature

1 tablespoon extra virgin olive oil

½ cup (packed) light brown sugar

½ cup (packed) dark brown sugar

**1.** Preheat the oven to 350°F. Grease a 13 x 9-inch baking pan with softened butter.

**2.** In a medium saucepan, bring the dates, water, dark chocolate and sugar to a boil. Reduce to simmer and stir occasionally, until the mixture thickens and becomes a spreadable paste. Cool for 10 minutes.

**3.** While the date mixture cools, place the spelt flour, oats, nuts, black caraway seeds, salt and baking soda in a large bowl. Whisk to combine, and set aside.

**4.** In a stand mixer fitted with a paddle attachment (or using a hand mixer), cream the butter and oil with the light and dark brown sugars until light and fluffy, 3 to 4 minutes. Turn the machine off, add the flour mixture and mix on low until just combined.

**5.** Firmly press half of the dough into the bottom of the prepared baking pan, covering it completely from corner to corner, filling in any cracks with more dough. Using an offset spatula, spread the date paste over the dough in an even layer. Crumble the remaining dough on top of the date paste, and press down slightly so that it sticks.

**6.** Bake for 33 to 35 minutes, or until the crumble is lightly golden brown.

**7.** Cool completely before cutting the bars into 15, approximately 3 x 2½-inch rectangles (or whatever size you prefer).

### Get Creative

**The Truly Caribbean-Inspired Variation**

Using the same method, create a crust with 1½ cups all-purpose flour, 1½ cups rolled oats, ¾ cup unsweetened shredded coconut, 1 teaspoon salt, ½ teaspoon baking soda, ½ cup light brown sugar, ½ cup dark brown sugar and ½ cup (1 stick) + 3 tablespoons butter. Instead of dates and chocolate, simply cut guava paste (available at most grocery stores or online) into ¼-inch-thick slices and layer them over the top of the bottom crust. Crumble the remaining dough on top as in the main recipe, then bake following the main recipe instructions.

# GOOEY HONEY BLONDIES

*Yield: one 8 x 8-inch pan, cut into 16 squares*

*Agatha and I love blondies for their in-between cookie and brownie texture, and for how easy they are to make (no machines, 1 whisk, 1 spatula). The honey in this recipe caramelizes in the oven and makes the blondies super ooey and gooey, just how we like them.*

Softened unsalted butter and all-purpose flour, for preparing the baking pan

1 stick + 2 tablespoons (5 ounces) unsalted butter

½ cup (packed) light brown sugar

½ cup (packed) dark brown sugar

¼ cup honey

1 large egg, at room temperature

1 teaspoon salt

1 teaspoon vanilla extract

1 cup + 2 tablespoons all-purpose flour

½ cup chocolate chips*

⅓ cup chopped raw pecans

*\*We prefer chocolate with 60 percent cocoa content or higher. If you are a chocolate lover, increase to ⅔ cup chocolate chips.*

1. Preheat the oven to 350°F. Grease an 8 x 8-inch baking pan with softened butter and dust the pan with flour.

2. In a small saucepan over low heat (or in a small, microwave-safe bowl in a microwave oven), melt the butter and set aside to cool.

3. In a large bowl, whisk together the melted butter, sugars, honey, egg, salt and vanilla extract until smooth. Add the flour and chocolate chips, and mix together with a wooden spoon or a rubber spatula.

4. Spread the batter in the prepared baking pan. Smooth out the top and edges, and then top with the pecans.

5. Bake for 25 minutes, or until the center is just set and the edges are barely golden. The blondies will be fully set when cool.

6. Cool completely before cutting the blondies into 16, 2 x 2-inch squares.

# COCONUT, CHOCOLATE &
# BROWN BUTTER BLONDIES

*Yield: one 8 x 8-inch pan, cut into 16 squares*

*Another quick and delicious blondie recipe. Be sure to taste the dough; it's heavenly.*

1 stick + 2 tablespoons (5 ounces)
unsalted butter + more,
for greasing the baking pan

1¼ cups all-purpose flour

1¼ cups unsweetened
shredded coconut

1¼ cups chocolate chips

¼ teaspoon salt

1 cup (packed) dark brown sugar

¼ cup sugar

1 large egg, at room temperature

2 teaspoons vanilla extract

**1.** Preheat the oven to 350°F. Liberally grease an 8 x 8-inch baking pan with softened butter.

**2.** In a saucepan over medium-low heat, melt the butter and continue to heat it until it crackles and foams. Once the foam begins to subside, the butter solids will quickly begin to brown on the bottom of the saucepan. Stir continuously with a wooden spoon to scrape browned bits off the bottom of the saucepan. Once the butter is nutty brown in color, remove it from the heat and cool. Do not let the butter burn. (See Brown Butter Process on page 133.)

**3.** In a large bowl, while the butter cools, whisk together the flour, coconut, chocolate chips and salt.

**4.** Once the butter is at room temperature, pour it into a large bowl and then whisk in the sugars, egg and vanilla extract.

**5.** Add the dry mixture to the wet mixture. With a rubber spatula, mix until just combined.

**6.** Pour the batter into the prepared baking pan and press into the pan with a spatula. Smooth the top.

**7.** Bake for 20 to 22 minutes, or until just set. The center will still be soft and may appear undercooked, but the blondies will set completely once out of the oven. Be sure not to overbake.

**8.** Cool completely before cutting the blondies into 16, 2 x 2-inch squares.

### Get Creative

Not a coconut fan? Omit the coconut, and replace it with ¾ cup rolled oats.

# BROWN BUTTER PROCESS

**01** Place the butter in a saucepan over medium-low heat to melt.

**02** Continue to heat the butter, stirring often, until it crackles and foams.

**03** When the foam begins to subside, the butter solids will quickly begin to brown. Stir vigorously with a wooden spoon, scraping browned bits off the bottom of the saucepan.

**04** When the butter is nutty brown in color, remove it from the heat and cool. Do not let the butter burn.

# PEANUT BUTTER & OAT GRANOLA BARS

*Yield: one 13 x 9-inch pan, cut into 15 bars*

*We have several regulars who order this granola bar every single morning and have done so since we opened our shop in Greenpoint. Hearty, fruity and nutty, these are a great way to start the day.*

Softened unsalted butter or nonstick cooking spray, for greasing the baking pan

4 cups gluten-free oats

1½ teaspoons ground cinnamon

1½ teaspoons baking soda

1 teaspoon ground ginger

½ teaspoon salt

½ cup chocolate chips (any kind)

½ cup unsweetened shredded coconut

½ cup dried sour cherries

8 tablespoons (1 stick, 4 ounces) unsalted butter, at room temperature

1⅓ cups (packed) dark brown sugar

¼ cup sugar

3 large eggs, at room temperature

1½ cups peanut butter*

1 teaspoon vanilla extract

Coarse sea salt, for garnish

*(We prefer Skippy)*

1. Preheat the oven to 350°F. Grease a 13 x 9-inch baking pan with softened butter or nonstick cooking spray.

2. In a large bowl, whisk together the oats, cinnamon, baking soda, ginger and salt. Set aside.

3. In a small bowl, combine the chocolate chips, coconut and dried cherries. Set aside.

4. In the bowl of a stand mixer fitted with a paddle attachment (or using a hand mixer), cream the butter with the sugars on medium-high until fluffy, about 3 minutes. Add the eggs, one at a time, and then beat for 30 seconds until smooth.

5. Scrape down the sides of the bowl with a rubber spatula. Add the peanut butter and vanilla extract, and mix on low until incorporated. Scrape down the sides of the bowl again, add the oat mixture and mix on the lowest speed for 2 minutes, allowing the oats to fully incorporate.

6. Scrape down the sides of the bowl again, and add the chocolate chips, coconut and dried cherries. Mix on low until well combined, about 30 seconds, and then scrape down the sides of the bowl one more time. Give the dough a final 10-second mix on low.

7. Remove the bowl from the machine, and transfer the dough into the prepared baking pan. Smooth the top with a spatula (an offset spatula works best), ensuring that the dough is evenly distributed in the baking dish.

8. Sprinkle the dough with coarse sea salt, and bake for 25 minutes, or until the top is golden and the center is just set.

9. Cool completely before cutting the bars into 15, approximately 3 x 2½-inch rectangles (or whatever size you prefer).

# CAKES & CUPCAKES

*Agatha* ❖ Whether it's out of a box, fresh from a bakery or homemade, the gift of a cake is guaranteed to make anyone's day. In fact, we think—because of how long they take to make, and how tricky they can be to assemble—that cake is the highest honor one can bestow upon a friend. More than once, I've spent hours in the middle of a heat wave making a cake in my tiny kitchen, before speed walking it across twenty-five city blocks while trying to prevent it from melting all over my clothes. But be forewarned: Once you take the plunge and start baking cakes for your friends, there's no turning back. They'll love you for it, and your closest circle might even come to expect it for every occasion. I speak from experience.

In my twenties, I spent countless hours reading about, experimenting with and eating cakes. I made them for birthdays, graduations and even weddings. I was dubbed the "cake queen," a title that I happily accepted. In fact, on that fateful night when I met Erin, my contribution to our book club dinner was Pistachio Cardamom Cupcakes with Dark Chocolate Ganache (see recipe on page 151). I like to think that was how I wooed her (she would agree).

When Erin and I first started experimenting with cakes for Ovenly, we discovered the beauty of the assembly process and naturally gravitated toward a tag-team baking style. After the layers were baked and cooled, I would slice off any uneven parts, and then Erin would evenly fill and crumb coat them. I liked to slather on the thick coating of buttercream; Erin had the steady hand for final smoothing and decorating; then I would clean up any imperfections. We even shared the packaging and delivery responsibilities. When we found ourselves schlepping towering tiered wedding cakes around town, Erin would be the designated driver and I would sit in the back of Wedgie, precariously clutching and balancing our precious cargo. Luckily, Erin is a pretty good driver.

Along the way we have learned better and safer ways to deliver cakes, but a collaborative assembly process is still how we operate our kitchen. This kind of teamwork makes it much more likely that all ingredients are measured and mixed correctly, and that our cakes are created both swiftly and precisely. Sure, all our cakes are simple enough to make on one's own, but when time is of the essence, as it always is at Ovenly, cooperation is the key.

The cake recipes that we offer in this cookbook are straightforward and easy to follow, so no assembly line is required. More important we guarantee that the results will be far more delicious, satisfying and natural than anything that you will find on your grocery store shelf. Our cake recipes draw inspiration from classic influences, but incorporate unexpected twists. Erin and I like to play around with citrus, freshly ground spices and different types of fillings and buttercream flavors, all of which reflect the sense of decadence that we are feeling in the moment. As you will see, these cakes are simple yet festive, unfussy yet graceful, great for both fancy celebrations and for cozy dinner parties.

When you're ready to hit the kitchen, be sure to put together a prep list of everything you will need prior to getting started. Gather and measure your ingredients before you begin so that you can move along fluidly from one task to the next. Also, since it's often impossible to taste the final product before it's served (the ultimate tease!), you'll have to become an expert at sampling the batter (yum) in order to make sure that everything is on track. We assure you that, with these recipes and some patience, you, too, can become a cake queen...or king.

# BLACK CHOCOLATE STOUT CAKE WITH SALTED CARAMEL CREAM CHEESE BUTTERCREAM

*Yield: one, two-layer 9-inch cake*

*This recipe is adapted from one in* Bon Appétit *and was one of the first Erin and I ever made together. It has become the go-to base of many of our chocolate cakes. We use Brooklyn Brewery's Black Chocolate Stout, which provides a subtly bitter, malted caramel flavor, but we encourage you to experiment with other stouts, as well.*

Softened unsalted butter and all-purpose flour, for preparing the baking pan

1½ cups Brooklyn Brewery Black Chocolate Stout, or other stout of choice

1½ cups (12 ounces) unsalted butter, cut into ½-inch pieces

1½ cups dark Dutch-process cocoa powder (see Essential Tools & Ingredients on page xxii)

3 cups all-purpose flour

2¾ cups sugar

¾ tablespoon baking soda

1½ teaspoons salt

1 cup sour cream (preferably full-fat)

3 large eggs, at room temperature

Salted Caramel Cream Cheese Buttercream (see recipe on page 183)

**1.** Preheat the oven to 350°F. Grease two 9-inch cake pans with butter and dust with flour. Line with parchment rounds and grease the rounds.

**2.** In a large heavy saucepan over medium heat, bring the stout and unsalted butter to a simmer. (You can also melt the butter in your oven or in a large, microwave-safe bowl in a microwave oven and then whisk in the beer.) Remove the stout-butter mixture from the heat, add the Dutch-process cocoa powder and whisk until the mixture is smooth. Let cool for 5 minutes.

**3.** While the stout-butter mixture cools, in a large bowl, whisk together the flour, sugar, baking soda and salt.

**4.** In a separate large bowl, whisk together the sour cream and eggs.

**5.** Add the stout-butter mixture to the egg mixture and whisk to combine. Then add the flour mixture, and combine with a rubber spatula until all the ingredients are incorporated and the batter is smooth, with no lumps. Be sure to scrape the bottom of the bowl to incorporate any dry flour bits.

**6.** Divide the batter equally between the prepared cake pans. Bake for 35 to 40 minutes, or until a toothpick inserted in the center of each layer comes out clean. Transfer to a rack to cool.

**7.** Frost the cake with Salted Caramel Cream Cheese Buttercream (see Cake Frosting Process on pages 146–147).

# BROOKLYN BLACKOUT CAKE

*Yield: one, two-layer 9-inch cake*

*The Ebinger Baking Company, an iconic baking institution from Brooklyn, is credited with first making the Brooklyn Blackout Cake, which recently had a resurgence in popularity in our neck of the woods. Being Brooklyn based ourselves, we decided to take a stab at our own version using our Salted Dark Chocolate Pudding. Instead of the traditional devil's food cake, we make our stout cake with almost-black, dark Dutch-process cocoa powder (see Essential Tools & Ingredients on page 9), which is richly bittersweet. Once our cake is baked, we add salted fudgy pudding into our base buttercream and then thickly layer it on the cake. A purely decadent dessert, this cake, we hope, is as memorable as its bold predecessor.*

---

**1.** Prepare the cake layers from the recipe for Black Chocolate Stout Cake on page 140.

**2.** Prepare the Dark Chocolate Pudding Buttercream recipe on page 183.

**3.** Once the cake layers have cooled, frost the cake with the Dark Chocolate Pudding Buttercream by following the process illustrated on pages 146–147.

# VARIATION: BLACKOUT CREAM CHEESE CUPCAKES

*Yield: 16 cupcakes*

*On days we are feeling a little less indulgent but are still looking for a good time, we make these little guys. The recipe shines on its own, requiring no frosting and no fuss. The tangy cream cheese swirled into this moist, dark chocolate cake is great for anyone with a morning sweet tooth. These cupcakes can easily double as muffins, perfectly paired with a cup of black coffee.*

---

Black Chocolate Stout Cake
(reduce recipe by half;
see recipe on page 140)

Cream Cheese Filling
for Cupcakes & Muffins
(see recipe on page 186)

Cream Cheese Topping
for Cupcakes & Muffins
(see recipe on page 186)

**1.** Preheat the oven to 375°F.

**2.** Line the wells of two 12-cup muffin/cupcake tins with baking cups. Using a large spoon, fill each well ⅓ full with Black Chocolate Stout Cake batter. Allow the batter to settle into the wells.

**3.** Spoon a heaping teaspoon of Cream Cheese Filling on top of the batter in the center of each well. Top with more batter, filling each well so that it is ⅔ full.

**4.** Spoon 1 teaspoon of Cream Cheese Topping over each filled well of the tin. Using a toothpick, delicately swirl the topping into the batter (topping will sink if you are heavy handed with this). Each cupcake should look marbled.

**5.** Bake for 22 to 24 minutes, or until a toothpick inserted in the center of a few cupcakes comes out clean. Place on a wire rack to cool.

# VANILLA BEAN CAKE WITH POMEGRANATE BUTTERCREAM

*Yield: one, two-layer 9-inch cake*

*Erin and I both think that the epitome of the perfect vanilla cake is Rose Levy Beranbaum's White Velvet Butter Cake from her book* The Cake Bible. *Inspired by her, we wanted to come up with our own vanilla cake that would be just as good. After several failed iterations, we passed the buck to our kitchen manager and baker, Johanna Jackson. She knocked it out of the park with this recipe. We hope Ms. Levy Beranbaum would be proud.*

Softened unsalted butter and all-purpose flour, for preparing the cake pans

4 cups cake flour, sifted

2 tablespoons baking powder

1 teaspoon salt

1½ cups heavy cream, at room temperature

1 cup sour cream, (preferably full-fat), at room temperature

Caviar from 2 vanilla bean pods

2½ cups sugar

1 pound (4 sticks, 16 ounces) softened unsalted butter

6 large eggs, at room temperature

Pomegranate Buttercream (see recipe on page 182)

**1.** Preheat the oven to 350°F. Grease two 9-inch cake pans with butter and dust with flour. Line with parchment rounds and grease the rounds.

**2.** In a large bowl, whisk together the cake flour, baking powder and salt. Set aside.

**3.** In a medium bowl, whisk together the heavy cream, sour cream and vanilla bean paste. Set aside.

**4.** In the bowl of a stand mixer fitted with a paddle attachment (or using a hand mixer), cream the sugar and unsalted butter together until light and fluffy, on medium speed, about 3 minutes. Add the eggs to the butter mixture, 1 at a time, turning the machine off to scrape down the sides of the bowl after each addition.

**5.** With the machine off, add a third of the flour mixture to the mixing bowl. Mix on low until the flour mixture is just incorporated. Add half of the sour cream mixture, and beat on medium-low until just incorporated. Add another third of the flour mixture and repeat the process, finishing with the remaining third of the flour mixture.

**6.** When all the ingredients have been added and appear almost combined, stop the mixer. Using a spatula, stir the batter and incorporate any remaining dry flour. Do not overmix.

**7.** Divide the batter equally between the prepared cake pans. Bake for 30 to 35 minutes, or until a toothpick inserted in the center of each layer comes out clean.

**8.** Let the layers cool for 20 minutes before removing them from the cake pans, and then let them cool completely.

**9.** Frost the cake with the Pomegranate Buttercream (see Cake Frosting Process on pages 146–147).

# CAKE FROSTING PROCESS

01  Using a serrated knife, level the cake layer by removing the crown. Repeat for each layer.

02  Place a large dollop of buttercream onto the cardboard round and spread it carefully. Press the bottom cake layer directly on the cardboard round, and place it on a revolving cake stand (see Essential Tools on page 4).

03  Using an offset spatula, spread the buttercream filling over the bottom layer, pushing the buttercream toward the edges of the cake. The buttercream should be about ½-inch thick.

04  Stack the next cake layer directly on top of the filling and gently press down to set it in place.

05  Spread the buttercream across the top layer of the cake, toward the edges of the cake.

06  Top the cake fully with frosting, spreading it into a thin and even layer. Do not worry if crumbs are in the frosting—this is called a crumb coat.

07  Place the cake in the freezer for at least 30 minutes.

08  Remove it to finish frosting. Spread a generous layer of buttercream over the top and sides of the cake. Even out the sides by holding the spatula upright, that is, at a 90-degree angle to the revolving cake stand. Slowly spin the revolving cake stand without lifting the spatula from the surface of the buttercream. As you turn the cake, add more buttercream and repeat the smoothing process.

09  Smooth the top of the cake with the edge of your spatula. (To make this step easier, dip your spatula in a glass of hot water and glide it across the surface of the buttercream.)

10  To create ridged sides, starting at the bottom of the cake, press the tip of your offset spatula gently into the buttercream. Hold it steady as you turn the cake and make ridges.

11  Hold a buttercream-filled pastry bag with a size 5 round tip at a 45-degree angle slightly above the surface of the cake. Pipe buttercream pearls around the border of the cake.

12  Have fun with decorations! Try using candied hearts (like we did), rose petals, or luster dust.

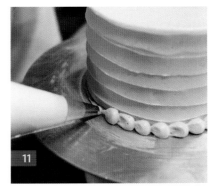

# VARIATION: VANILLA BEAN CAKE WITH FIG FILLING

*Yield: one, two-layer 9-inch cake*

Vanilla Bean Cake

(see recipe on page 144)

10 ounces dried Black Mission figs

1¾ cups orange juice

½ cup water

2 tablespoons vanilla extract

Buttercream Frosting Base Recipe
(see recipe on page 180)

**1.** Prepare the Vanilla Bean Cake.

**2.** Prepare the fig filling by removing the stems from the figs and cutting them in half. Place the fig halves in a medium saucepan with the orange juice, water and vanilla extract. Soak the figs for 15 minutes, and then heat the saucepan over medium heat until the mixture begins to boil, stirring occasionally. Reduce heat to simmer until the liquid is fully absorbed, about 15 minutes. Remove the figs from the heat and let cool.

**3.** In a food processor, puree the cooked figs until smooth and thick.

**4.** Spread the fig filling over the bottom cake layer. Place the top cake layer directly over the filling, and then frost the cake with the Buttercream Frosting (see recipe on page 180 and Cake Frosting Process on pages 146–147).

# PISTACHIO CAKE
# WITH LEMON CURD
# & LEMON BUTTERCREAM

*Yield: one, two-layer 9-inch cake*

*Our pistachio cardamom cake was such a hit that we wanted to make a gluten-free version of it so that our celiac/ wheat-allergic friends wouldn't miss out. The soft, delicate crumb makes this cake almost indistinguishable from the wheat flour-based version. Even your gluten-loving friends will love it and will never know the difference!*

Softened unsalted butter and all-purpose flour, for preparing the cake pans

2 cups gluten-free flour mix (see recipe on page 87)

2 cups ground pistachio meal (see note on grinding nuts and spices on page 11)

2 tablespoons fresh ground cardamom (see note on grinding nuts and spices on page 11)

1 tablespoon baking powder

¾ teaspoon xanthan gum

¾ teaspoon salt

2¼ cups sugar

3 sticks (24 tablespoons, 1½ cups) softened unsalted butter

Zest of 3 lemons

6 large eggs, at room temperature

1 cup sour cream (perferably full-fat)

¾ teaspoon vanilla extract

Lemon Curd (use 1 cup only; see recipe on page 192)

Lemon Buttercream (see recipe on page 180)

**1.** Preheat the oven to 350°F. Grease two 9-inch cake pans with butter and dust with flour. Line with parchment rounds and grease the rounds.

**2.** In a large bowl, mix together the gluten-free flour mix, pistachio meal, fresh ground cardamom, baking powder, xanthan gum and salt.

**3.** In the bowl of a stand mixer fitted with a paddle attachment (or using a hand mixer), cream the sugar, unsalted butter and lemon zest on medium-high until light and fluffy, about 2 to 3 minutes. Add the eggs and blend until well incorporated. Scrape down the sides of the bowl with a rubber spatula.

**4.** With the machine off, add the sour cream and vanilla extract to the egg mixture, and mix on medium-low until incorporated, about 30 seconds.

**5.** Add the flour mixture to the wet mixture. Mix until well incorporated.

**6.** Divide the batter equally between the 2 prepared cake pans. Bake for 25 to 35 minutes, or until a toothpick inserted in the center of each layer comes out clean. Let cool before removing the layers from the cake pans.

**7.** Once the layers are completely cool, use an offset spatula to smooth the 1 cup Lemon Curd on the bottom cake layer. Place the top layer directly over the bottom layer. Frost the cake with the Lemon Buttercream, leaving about an inch of space at the edges of the cake (see Cake Frosting Process on pages 146–147).

# PISTACHIO CARDAMOM CUPCAKES WITH DARK CHOCOLATE GANACHE

*Yield: 12 cupcakes*

*Exploring the unassuming Indian delis in the East Village for flavor inspiration has always been one of my favorite pastimes. The array of fragrant and exotic spices I encounter in them is so tempting that I often find myself unable to resist purchasing ridiculous amounts of mysterious pods, powders and dried flowers. I test this stuff in everything—pancakes, puddings, scones, you name it. In fact, one bag of brilliantly colored green cardamom pods became the star ingredient in these cupcakes. Buy the cardamom fresh, and grind it yourself (see note on grinding nuts and spices on page 11) for a real kick. We promise that taking that small extra step won't disappoint.*

1 cup ground pistachio meal (see note on grinding nuts and spices on page 11)

2 teaspoons fresh ground cardamom (see note on grinding nuts and spices on page 11)

1 cup all-purpose flour

2 teaspoons baking powder

½ teaspoon salt

1 cup sugar

10 tablespoons (5 ounces) unsalted butter, at room temperature

Zest of 1 lemon

3 large eggs, at room temperature

½ cup sour cream (preferably full-fat), at room temperature

½ teaspoon vanilla extract

Dark Chocolate Ganache (see recipe on page 187)

1 to 2 tablespoons chopped pistachios, for garnish

**1.** Preheat the oven to 350°F. Line the wells of a 12-cup cupcake tin with baking cups.

**2.** In a large bowl, whisk together the pistachio meal, fresh ground cardamom, flour, baking powder and salt. Set aside.

**3.** In the bowl of a stand mixer fitted with a paddle attachment (or using a hand mixer), cream the sugar, butter and lemon zest on medium-high until light and fluffy, about 2 to 3 minutes. With the machine running, add the eggs, 1 at a time, incorporating each egg into the batter before adding the next. Turn the machine off, and scrape down the sides of the bowl with a rubber spatula.

**4.** With the machine on low, add the sour cream and vanilla extract. Mix for 2 minutes, or until the batter is almost uniform.

**5.** Add the flour mixture to the bowl of the stand mixer, and then mix on low until just incorporated, about 1 minute. Remove the bowl from the mixer, and using a rubber spatula, give the batter 1 final mix, ensuring no dry flour is left at the bottom of the bowl.

**6.** Using a scoop or a large spoon, portion the batter evenly in the wells of the cupcake tin, filling each ⅔ full.

**7.** Bake for 18 minutes, or until a toothpick inserted in the center of a few cupcakes comes out clean. Place on a wire rack to cool.

**8.** Using a small offset spatula (or butter knife), place a large dollop of Dark Chocolate Ganache on each cupcake and smooth over in a circular motion from the center to the outer edges. For decoration, top each cupcake with the chopped pistachios.

# CHOCOLATE CHEESECAKE WITH SOUR CREAM TOPPING

*Yield: one 8-inch cake*

*Just like our recipes, Erin and I are the perfect partnership of sweet and savory. This airy, tangy and chocolaty cheesecake recipe was passed on to us by Mama Patinkin and reflects this balance. Erin says this was her all-time favorite dessert growing up, and she still loves it. The first time we made this cake together, I got hooked, too.*

### CRUST

6 tablespoons (3 ounces) unsalted butter

2 tablespoons sugar

1½ cups finely ground graham cracker crumbs (about 12 graham crackers, pulverized in a food processor or by hand)

### FILLING

2 cups (two 8-ounce packages) cream cheese, softened

1¼ cups sugar

½ cup unsweetened Dutch-process cocoa powder (see Essential Tools & Ingredients on page 9)

2 large eggs, at room temperature

1 teaspoon vanilla extract

Pinch of salt

### TOPPING

½ cup sour cream (full-fat or plain full-fat yogurt), at room temperature

2 tablespoons sugar

½ teaspoon vanilla extract

Pinch of salt

**1.** Prepare the crust. In a small saucepan over low heat (or in a small, microwave-safe bowl in a microwave oven), melt the butter and set aside to cool. Pour the butter into a large bowl and whisk in the sugar and then the graham cracker crumbs. Combine thoroughly.

**2.** Press the graham cracker mixture into the bottom of an 8-inch springform pan and a third of the way up the sides. Freeze the crust for at least 30 minutes to set.

**3.** Preheat the oven to 375°F.

**4.** Prepare the filling. Beat the cream cheese in the bowl of a standing mixer fitted with a paddle attachment (or using a hand mixer) on medium speed, until fluffy, about 2 minutes. Turn the machine off, scrape down the sides of the bowl, and add 1¼ cups sugar and the cocoa. Mix on low for 10 seconds. Increase the speed to medium-high and beat until smooth, about 1 minute.

**5.** Scrape down the sides of the bowl, and with the machine off, add the eggs, vanilla extract and salt. Beat the filling on medium-low speed for about 10 seconds, then increase the speed to medium-high until fluffy and silky smooth, about 30 more seconds.

**6.** Remove the prepared crust from the freezer, and pour the filling into the springform pan. Smooth the top with a spatula, and bake for 30 minutes.

**7.** While the cheesecake bakes, prepare the topping. In a large bowl, whisk together the sour cream, sugar, vanilla extract and salt.

**8.** Remove the cheesecake from the oven, leaving the oven at 375°F. Very carefully spoon the sour cream topping on the hot cake, and use a spatula to smooth it to form a thin, even layer over the top, being careful not to press too hard on the delicate, hot cake. Return the cheesecake to the oven, and bake for 30 to 40 minutes more, or until the top looks set.

**9.** Cool the cheesecake completely at room temperature, and then chill it thoroughly (for at least 6 hours) before serving.

# BAKING FOR
# THE HOLIDAYS

*Erin* ❖ Back in 2010, Agatha and I had one PR goal: to be featured on *Daily Candy*. By networking our butts off, we finagled the food editor's email and office address. Looking fashionable, and with a box of blue cheese–pecan scones, honey-almond caramel corn and caramel-bacon hot tarts in hand, Agatha took the subway to SoHo to personally deliver our gift. When she arrived, a secretary greeted her at the office doors, accepted the box and promised that it would get into the hands of the right person.

At this point, we had been delivering our wares to various local coffee shops for some time. We had quickly learned that if the manager or owner didn't directly receive the samples, they would mysteriously disappear—presumably into an unintended recipient's stomach. In the case of *Daily Candy,* Agatha and I suspected that by the time she returned to Brooklyn, the interns and the administrative staff would have scarfed down our scones and snacks, and that would be that.

Much to our surprise, we received this email later in the day:

*Dearest Agatha and Erin,*

*My thighs are covered in buttery, flaky crust remnants, and I will lick them up later. That's just how much I loved your confections.*

*My coworkers and I Hoovered the entire box of scones and Hot Tarts, and I am withholding the other treats for later in the afternoon so we don't all die.*

*I'd love to work with you on a story. Are you doing anything special/new for the holidays? A party pack? Something like that.*

*Thanks again for the samples—they were immensely enjoyed and appreciated.*

*Best,*

*Erin W.*

Agatha and I hadn't much planned for the holidays, but after that email, we immediately got to work on a special Ovenly "party pack," which we decided to sell on our website. This was a few months after we had officially launched Ovenly. We had only three clients—Veronica People's Club, Brooklyn Brewery and Bedford Hill Coffee Bar—and were still paying the bills with our full-time office jobs. Our website wasn't fully functional. We had no e-commerce store. And we had access to a commercial kitchen just a few days a week. Oh, did I mention the fact that we had never, ever packaged and shipped our treats anywhere?

*No matter,* we thought. *This will be a piece of cake!* (Bakery pun intended.)

We responded to Erin W.'s kind email with a description of the contents of our hastily assembled holiday box and informed her that they would be available for order after Thanksgiving. No response came. We figured that *Daily Candy* had forgotten about us as soon as their sugar highs wore off. But because Agatha and I actually liked the idea of doing something special for the holidays, we decided to offer the "party pack" to our friends and family, anyway.

Orders trickled in from our loved ones—nothing overwhelming. Then, out of nowhere, right before Thanksgiving, *Daily Candy* published a last-minute holiday guide in which they recommended Ovenly gifts to their readers. The mention was brief: "A festive arrangement ($30–$50) of cinnamon-, pepper-, and cumin-laced pistachio brittle, spicy bacon popcorn coated in a Brooklyn Brewery Pennant Ale caramel sauce, and more…" The exposure was compounded when, on the same day, *Daily Candy*'s national editor proclaimed us a "best trend for 2010." In the eighteen hours that followed, we received over three hundred orders.

Agatha and I went into freak-out mode and started churning out caramel corn and brittle. My dining room table morphed into a packaging production line, and my living room became a party pack warehouse. To fill orders, we enlisted the help of Agatha's boyfriend at the time and a bevy of other friends. We taught them how to don a hairnet and to heat seal cellophane bags accurately so that they wouldn't melt. In the five days we had to fill orders, we slept a total of maybe six hours.

There were a lot of mistakes—one of which compelled me to hand deliver an apology card to a loft in the East Village. But fill the orders we did. And, despite the absolute mayhem, that first holiday started a trend, inspiring us to invent new recipes (and to plan ahead) for the following seasons. The next year we developed a line of specialty pies for Thanksgiving and rum cream–filled eggnog cookies for Christmastime. After that, we got more creative: booze–soaked fig blondies for the New Year, citrus–dried apricot hamantaschen specials for Purim and prune jam–filled *pączki* for Easter.

This chapter includes all those, plus some others that we hope will help to put you in the holiday spirit (and not a frenzied one).

# EGGNOG SANDWICH COOKIES

*Yield: approximately 30 cookies (depending on cookie cutter size)*

*This sparkly Christmas cookie has become a holiday standard at Ovenly. The rum cream filling combined with cinnamon and nutmeg in the sugar cookie is reminiscent of everyone's favorite wintertime cocktail.*

### SUGAR COOKIES

2 cups confectioners' sugar, sifted

16 tablespoons (8 ounces) unsalted butter, at room temperature

2 tablespoons light corn syrup

2 teaspoons ground cinnamon

1 teaspoon freshly grated nutmeg

1 teaspoon vanilla extract

¾ teaspoon salt

¼ teaspoon ground cloves

1 large egg, at room temperature

3 tablespoons rum

2 teaspoons baking powder

3½ cups all-purpose flour + more for dusting

Sanding sugar, for decorating the cookies

### CREAM FILLING

3 cups confectioners' sugar, sifted

¼ cup rum

¼ cup heavy cream + more for thinning

**1.** In the bowl of a stand mixer fitted with a paddle attachment (or using a hand mixer), cream together the confectioners' sugar, butter and corn syrup until very fluffy and light in color, about 3 minutes. Add the cinnamon, nutmeg, vanilla extract, salt and cloves and beat until combined, about 30 seconds more.

**2.** In a small bowl, whisk together the egg and rum, and then stir in the baking powder until it dissolves completely. With the mixer on low, add the egg mixture and mix until barely incorporated. Turn the mixer off and add the flour. With the machine on low, mix until the flour is well incorporated and the dough is smooth, about 1 minute.

**3.** Divide the dough in half, and form it into 2 disks, each 6 inches in diameter. Wrap each in plastic wrap and refrigerate for at least 1 hour, or until the dough is firm.

**4.** Line 3 rimmed sheet pans (if you do not have 3, you will have to bake these cookies in batches) with parchment paper. Preheat the oven to 350°F. Lightly flour your work surface and rolling pin, and sprinkle the dough with extra flour to prevent it from sticking.

**5.** Roll the dough to a thickness of ¼ inch, lifting it as you roll and flipping it over a few times to prevent it from sticking to the work surface. With a cookie cutter (we usually use a 1½-inch round cutter or a small glass), cut the dough into the desired shape and transfer the cookies to the prepared sheet pans (these cookies do not expand much, so you can bake 20 per pan). Reroll and cut any leftover dough.

**6.** Place them in the freezer (you can stack the pans in the freezer by placing parchment in between each. If you do not have 3 pans you can stack cookies in single layers, lining parchment in between each layer) for 15 minutes before baking. This will allow the cookies to retain their shape.

**7.** Sprinkle each cookie with sanding sugar, and bake the cookies pan by pan for 8 to 10 minutes, or until they are slightly golden on the edges. Let the cookies cool completely before assembling.

**8.** While the cookies cool, prepare the cream filling. In a large bowl, whisk all the filling ingredients together thoroughly until a thick, but spreadable paste forms. Thin the filling with cream if it is too dry.

**9.** Spoon a dollop of the cream filling on the center of a cookie and top it with another cookie, pressing down lightly to ensure that the filling spreads evenly in between but not beyond the cookie edges. Repeat this process until all the cookies are filled.

# BOOZY FIG BLONDIES

*Yield: one 9 x 13-inch pan, cut into 15 bars*

Softened unsalted butter and all-purpose flour, for preparing the baking pan

¾ cup chopped (into ¼-inch pieces) dried Black Mission figs

½ cup dried currants

1 cup whiskey or bourbon

1 cup (8 ounces, 2 sticks) unsalted butter

2 cups all-purpose flour

1½ teaspoons baking powder

½ teaspoon salt

¼ teaspoon ground black pepper

¼ teaspoon ground cloves

2 cups (packed) light brown sugar

2 large eggs, at room temperature

2 teaspoons vanilla extract

½ cup unsweetened shredded coconut

½ cup roughly chopped raw pistachio nuts

**1.** Place the figs and currants in a medium heatproof bowl.

**2.** In a small saucepan, bring the whiskey to a low boil over medium heat. Pour the hot liquor over the figs and currants. Let them soak for at least 1 hour, and then drain the fruit in a colander or mesh sieve placed over a bowl and reserve the whiskey for later use.

**3.** Preheat the oven to 350°F. Grease a 9 x 13-inch baking pan with softened butter and dust the pan with flour.

**4.** In a small saucepan over low heat (or in a small, microwave-safe bowl in a microwave oven), melt the butter and set aside to cool.

**5.** In a medium bowl, whisk together the flour, baking powder, salt, pepper and cloves.

**6.** Pour the melted butter into a large bowl, and add the brown sugar. Whisk vigorously to combine. Add the eggs, vanilla extract and reserved whiskey, and whisk until smooth.

**7.** Add the flour mixture to the butter-egg mixture. Use a spatula to mix until just combined, and then add the booze-soaked figs, currants and coconut. Stir until fully incorporated.

**8.** Spread the batter in the prepared baking pan, and sprinkle evenly with the pistachios.

**9.** Bake for 33 to 35 minutes, or until a toothpick inserted in the center of the bars comes out clean. Cool completely before cutting the blondies into 15, approximately 3 x 2½-inch, rectangles (or whatever size you prefer).

# APRICOT ORANGE HAMANTASCHEN

## *Yield: 12 cookies*

*Hamantaschen are traditionally eaten on the Jewish holiday Purim, a celebration of freedom and victory over evil that, as Joan Nathan, the world's foremost expert on Jewish cookery, points out, places more of an emphasis on festivities and delights (read "drinking and eating to excess") than any other Jewish holiday. We like that type of tradition. The buttery dough is very delicate and has a tendency to flake apart if chilled for too long, so roll it out after just 15 minutes of refrigeration. If the dough is too firm when you remove it from the fridge, let it sit at room temperature for 10 minutes before rolling.*

### DOUGH

1 cup (8 ounces, 2 sticks) cold unsalted butter

2¼ cups all-purpose flour, sifted

1 cup confectioners' sugar, sifted

½ teaspoon salt

2 large egg yolks

2 tablespoons honey

### APRICOT ORANGE FILLING

2 cups chopped (into about ¼-inch pieces) dried apricots (preferably Turkish)

1 cup water

¼ cup orange juice

¼ cup sugar

Zest of 1 orange

Zest of 1 lemon

½ teaspoon salt

### EGG WASH

1 large egg yolk

1 teaspoon water

1. Line a rimmed sheet pan with parchment paper.

2. Cut the butter into ¼- to ½-inch cubes. In a large bowl, whisk together the flour, confectioners' sugar and salt. Using a pastry cutter, cut the butter into the flour mixture until it has a cornmeal-like consistency.

3. Make a well in the center of the flour mixture, and add the egg yolks and honey. Stir with a spoon until blended (you can also use your hands to blend). Pat the dough into a 6-inch round disk, and refrigerate for 15 minutes.

4. While the dough chills, make the apricot-orange jam. Place all the jam ingredients in a medium saucepan. Bring to a boil over medium-high heat, stirring often, and then reduce the heat and simmer for 15 minutes, or until the apricots are tender and the water has mostly dissolved. Stir occasionally.

5. Transfer the mixture to a food processor, scraping out all the juices from the saucepan, and pulse until the apricots form a thick paste. Let the jam cool before using.

6. Remove the dough from the refrigerator, and roll it to a thickness of ⅛ to ¼ inch. Then cut it into 2-inch rounds with a cookie cutter or a glass. Reroll and recut any excess dough.

7. Place a heaping teaspoon of jam directly in the center of each round of dough. Fold up 2 edges of a round and pinch them together to make a corner of a triangle (see process on pages 164–165). Fold up the third edge to create the remaining corners of the triangle. Ensure that the dough is pinched together well. Otherwise, it can pop open while it bakes. Repeat this process until all the cookies are folded.

8. Place the cookies on the prepared rimmed sheet pan, and freeze for 10 minutes.

9. Preheat the oven to 375°F. Make the egg wash by whisking the egg yolk and water together until smooth.

10. Remove the cookies from the freezer, and brush them with the egg wash. Bake for 13 to 15 minutes, or until just golden, turning the rimmed sheet pan halfway through baking.

## HAMANTASCHEN PROCESS

01 Roll out the dough to ⅛- to ¼-inch thick, and cut it into rounds using a 2-inch cookie cutter. Reroll any scraps, and cut these into rounds, too.

02 Using a spoon or a scoop, place a heaping teaspoon of filling in the center of each round.

03 Fold the dough in toward the filling on 3 sides.

04 Pinch the corners together firmly. These can pop open, so make sure the dough holds together well.

05 Brush with egg wash before baking.

01

02

03

04

05

**Get Creative**

You can fill hamantaschen with any of your favorite jams—homemade or store-bought. Just ensure that you simmer the jam for 5 minutes to thicken it, and then let it cool completely before using.

# *PĄCZKI* WITH PRUNE BUTTER

*Yield: approximately 20* pączki

*I kinda hate doughnuts. An unfortunate mishap involving a cruller at a gas station in rural Wisconsin when I was ten years old scarred me for life. But then came* pączki. *Pączki (pronounced ponch-ky) are served in Poland on Easter, and the first year we met, incredulous that I hated doughnuts, Agatha bought one for me from a local Greenpoint bakery. Hot, crispy, tender and sweet, she proved to me that doughnuts could be awesome (though I'm still cruller averse). For our cookbook, Agatha's dad, Zdzislaw, sent us a recipe from Agatha's great aunt, with a serious note reminding us that* pączki *are good to make no matter the time of year. In homage to Eastern Europe, we've stuffed our version with prune butter, but any fruit spread will do.*

1½ cups whole milk + more for thinning the dough

3 tablespoons + 2¼ teaspoons (1¼ ounces) active dry yeast

1 tablespoon + 4 tablespoons + ½ teaspoon sugar

½ cup + 5¾ cups all-purpose flour, sifted + more for kneading

1½ tablespoons unsalted butter

4 egg yolks

¼ cup rum or *spirytus* (neutral spirits)

3 cups safflower or peanut oil, for frying + more for oiling the bowl

Prune butter or homemade jam (see recipe on page 193), for filling

Confectioners' sugar, for dusting

**1.** Heat the whole milk in a small saucepan over medium-low heat, to 110°F to 115°F.

**2.** Dissolve the yeast in the warm milk in a medium bowl. Add 1 tablespoon of the sugar and a ½ cup of the flour, whisk together thoroughly and set aside.

**3.** In a small saucepan or in a small, microwave-safe bowl in a microwave oven, melt the butter and set aside to cool.

**4.** In a separate small bowl, vigorously whisk together the remaining 4 tablespoons and ½ teaspoon sugar, egg yolks and rum until frothy.

**5.** Place the remaining 5¾ cups flour in a large bowl. Whisk the yeast mixture again, and pour it over the flour. Add the egg mixture, and mix with a wooden spoon or a spatula until the dough just starts to come together. Add the melted butter, and combine until smooth.

**6.** Liberally flour a work surface, and turn the dough out onto it. Knead the dough until it comes together and no longer sticks to your hands when worked. If the dough seems dry, add a little more milk and knead. If the dough seems too wet, add a bit more flour.

**7.** Lightly oil a large bowl and place the dough in it. Cover with a towel or plastic wrap, and let rise in a warm area until it doubles in size (about 1 hour).

**8.** Punch the dough down and separate it into 2 balls. Flour your work surface again, and roll the first ball into a disk about ½-inch thick.

**9.** Using a 3-inch cookie cutter or an inverted drinking glass, cut rounds out of the dough. Set the scraps of dough aside.

**10.** Place 1 tablespoon prune butter in the center of 1 of the rounds. Top it with another round, and pinch the seams with your fingers to seal the edges. Then bring together the edges of the dough on 1 side to create a sphere (see process on pages 168–169), and pinch to make a new seam. Reshape each ball with your hands to re-form it into a fluffy round shape. Repeat this process for the remaining rounds. Set each filled *pączki* on a floured surface.

**11.** Repeat this process with the remaining ball of dough. Reroll all the scraps of dough, and repeat this process again.

**12.** Let the filled *pączki* rise for 20 minutes, or until fluffy.

**13.** After the *pączki* have risen for 15 minutes, heat the oil in a heavy-bottomed steel or cast-iron skillet to 350°F on a candy thermometer, and line a large plate or a cooling rack with paper towels.

**14.** Once the oil is ready, use a slotted spoon to carefully place 3 or 4 *pączki* in the hot oil. Fry for 45 seconds, or until golden brown on 1 side. Flip the *pączki* and fry on the other side until golden brown, about 25 to 35 seconds.

**15.** Remove the *pączki* from the oil immediately and transfer to the prepared plate or cooling rack.

**16.** Let the *pączki* cool completely. Using a fine-mesh sieve, sprinkle them with confectioners' sugar. Serve immediately.

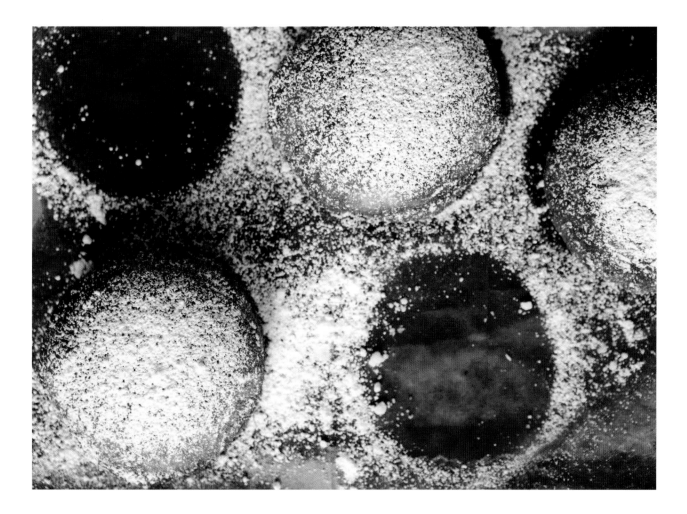

## *PĄCZKI* PROCESS

01 Once the prepared dough is rolled out, use a 3-inch cookie cutter or an inverted drinking glass to cut rounds out of the dough.

02 Place the filling in the center of 1 of the rounds.

03 Top it with another round.

04 Repeat this process with the remaining rounds.

05 Pinch just the ends with your fingers to seal the edges securely.

06 Reshape the *pączki* so that they are fluffy and round, and set them aside to rise for 20 minutes.

07 Heat the oil in a skillet to 350°F. Fry the *pączki* until they are golden brown on each side.

08 Remove the *pączki* from the oil and transfer them to a plate or a cooling rack lined with paper towels to drain.

09 Using a fine-mesh sieve, sprinkle the cooled *pączki* with confectioners' sugar.

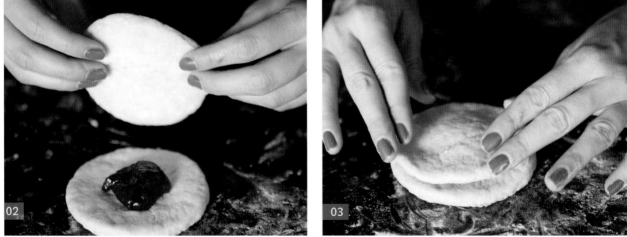

**Note**

To ensure your pączki are perfectly fried but not greasy, heat your oil to 350°F before frying and reheat it to 350°F between batches.

**9.** Bake the cookies until they are very light golden in color, 15 to 17 minutes, rotating the pans halfway through baking. Cool the cookies by placing the rimmed sheet pans directly on racks. Do not remove cookies from the rimmed sheet pans while hot as they can break apart.

**10.** While the cookies bake and cool, prepare the filling. Place the jam in a medium saucepan and bring it to a boil over low to medium heat, stirring occasionally to prevent burning. After the jam boils, lower the heat and simmer it steadily, allowing it to reduce, for about 5 minutes, or until it is slightly sticky and no longer watery.

**11.** As each batch cools, turn half the cookies upside down so that the flat sides face upward. Put about a heaping teaspoon of the reduced jam on each of the upturned cookies and then top each with 1 of the remaining cookies, putting the flat side down. Continue until all the cookies have been filled with jam.

## Get Creative

Use 1 cup of whatever nut you prefer in this recipe. We find that walnuts, hazelnuts or pecans taste best.

# FILLINGS, FROSTINGS & SAUCES

*Agatha* ❖ When I was a child, walking through the grocery store aisles captivated me, and exploring that giant labyrinth of possibilities made me giddy. The aisles that I gravitated toward were, of course, (1) the candy aisle, (2) the ice cream (and toppings) aisle and (3) the baking aisle. I would peruse the shelves, salivate at the sight of squeezable Smucker's Magic Shell and make a mental list of the essential ingredients for making the perfect ice cream sundae. The list varied week to week, but it never failed to include chocolate fudge, caramel sauce and pudding mix. When I got home, I would dump all of them into a giant bowl of Neapolitan ice cream and swish everything around until I found my desired consistency: lumpy soup.

# FLOURLESS CHOCOLATE CAKE

*Yield: one 9-inch cake*

*I've been making this cake for Passover for at least a decade. The combination of brown sugars and chocolate adds a lot of depth to this rich dessert. Perfect for Seder or any after-dinner occasion.*

---

Softened unsalted butter
for greasing the cake pan

14 tablespoons (7 ounces)
unsalted butter

1¾ cups (14 ounces) high-quality
dark chocolate*

6 large eggs, at room temperature

½ cup sugar

¼ cup (packed) light brown sugar

¼ cup (packed) dark brown sugar

1 teaspoon vanilla extract

*\*We prefer chocolate with
60 percent cocoa
content or higher.*

**1.** Preheat the oven to 350°F. Grease a 9-inch cake pan (with at least 2-inch sides), with softened butter, and line with a parchment round.

**2.** Cut the butter into ¼- to ½-inch cubes. Place the chocolate and butter in a medium metal bowl. Place the bowl over a saucepan filled with 1 inch of cold water to create a double boiler. Melt the chocolate and butter over medium-low heat, stirring often with a rubber spatula, until completely smooth. Remove from the heat and let cool. (You can also melt the mixture in a microwave-safe bowl by heating in a microwave oven for 20 seconds. After 20 seconds, stir and repeat until fully melted.)

**3.** In a large bowl, whisk together the eggs, sugars and vanilla extract until fully blended.

**4.** Add the cooled chocolate mixture to the egg mixture, and whisk until combined and smooth.

**5.** Pour the batter into the prepared 9-inch cake pan. Place a small, clean kitchen towel in a larger pan (a 12-inch cake pan works well here), and place the filled 9-inch cake pan on top of it. Fill the larger cake pan with water until it reaches halfway up the side of the 9-inch cake pan to create a water bath. Tightly cover the entire 2 pans with aluminum foil. (The towel will prevent the cake from slipping when you remove it from the oven.)

**6.** Place the cake in the oven, and bake for 85 to 90 minutes. To check for doneness, lightly touch the top of the cake with your finger. The cake is ready when your finger comes away clean. Be careful not to burn yourself when removing the aluminum foil, as there will be a lot of steam.

**7.** Once the cake is done, remove the aluminum foil, and using hot pads, take it out of the water bath. Let cool for at least 20 minutes before inverting it onto a cake plate or a waxed cardboard round. Cool completely before serving.

**Get Creative**

· Try adding 1½ teaspoons ground cinnamon or another of your favorite spices to the cake.

· Drizzle the cake with Salted Caramel Sauce (see recipe on page 190) before serving.

# SWEET POTATO & DRIED FIG TART

*Yield: one 9-inch tart*

*Maybe it's because of our Eastern European backgrounds, or maybe it's just because they're so delicious, but Agatha and I both love the sticky-chewy sweetness of dried Black Mission figs. Doused in cognac and reduced, they become fragrant and even more heavenly. Featuring figs paired with the earthy goodness of sweet potatoes, this tart has become our go-to for Thanksgiving. Any figs you don't use in the tart can be served on the side. If you are not a fan of figs, you can use a dried fruit of your preference in the same ratio as the figs in this recipe. Dried currants or prunes make wonderful substitutions.*

**BOOZY FIGS (see inset)**

**CRUST**

Pâte Brisée (see recipe on page 98; substitute ½ cup rye flour for ½ cup of the all-purpose flour)

Cream and sugar, for brushing on the crust

**SWEET POTATO FILLING**

2 large sweet potatoes or yams

1 cup heavy cream + more for brushing

3 large eggs

½ cup (packed) light brown sugar

2 teaspoons ground cinnamon

1 teaspoon vanilla extract

½ teaspoon salt

¼ teaspoon freshly grated nutmeg

Zest of 1 orange

Sugar, for sprinkling

**1.** Prepare the figs and set aside.

**2.** Prepare the Pâte Brisée recipe, using rye flour substitution. (You will only need 1 crust, so freeze the other for later use.)

**3.** Remove 1 disk of the Pâte Brisée from the refrigerator 10 minutes before rolling. Roll out the disk to a thickness of ¼ inch (about 12 inches in diameter) so that it is big enough to line the bottom of a 9-inch pie pan. Press the dough into the pie pan, and then chill it in the refrigerator for at least 30 minutes, or freeze it for 10 minutes (or up to overnight) before using. (See Double Crust Process on pages 104–105.)

## BOOZY FIGS

8 cardamom pods

4 whole peppercorns

2 whole cloves

2 cups Black Mission figs, stemmed and cut into ¼-inch pieces

¾ cup whiskey

¾ cup water

½ cup sugar

1 teaspoon vanilla extract

Zest of 1 orange

**1.** Crack the cardamom pods with the back of a knife or in a mortar and pestle. Fill an empty tea bag with the cracked cardamom pods, peppercorns and cloves. Tie the tea bag together with a piece of butcher's string.

**2.** In a medium saucepan, combine the tea bag and all the remaining ingredients. Bring to a boil, and then lower the heat and simmer until the whiskey and water have been almost completely absorbed by the figs, 15 to 20 minutes. Once the liquid is absorbed, toss the bouquet garni and let the figs cool.

**4.** Preheat the oven to 400°F. Line a rimmed sheet pan with aluminum foil.

**5.** Puncture the sweet potatoes all over with a fork. Bake them until tender on the prepared rimmed sheet pan, 45 to 50 minutes.

**6.** Let the sweet potatoes cool, and then cut them in half and scrape the insides into a medium bowl. Discard the skins. Mash the sweet potatoes until smooth with a fork or a potato masher (you can also puree them in a food processor). Measure out 2¼ cups of the mashed sweet potatoes, and reserve any leftover for another use.

**7.** In a mixing bowl, combine the cream, eggs, brown sugar, cinnamon, vanilla extract, salt, nutmeg and orange zest. Whisk together well. Add the mashed sweet potatoes and whisk until very smooth.

**8.** Remove the crust from the freezer, and brush the edges with cream. Sprinkle sugar on the crust, and then line the bottom of the pie pan with half of the boozy figs. Then fill it evenly with the sweet potato mixture.

**9.** Bake for 45 minutes, or until the sweet potato filling is puffy, golden and fully set. Let the tart cool completely. Serve with sweetened sour cream (¾ cup sour cream, ¼ teaspoon vanilla extract, 1 tablespoon sugar) or freshly whipped cream and reserved figs.

## Get Creative

Once the tart has cooled, spread ½ cup sugar evenly over the top. Using a torch, melt the sugar to form a crispy shell. Allow the tart brûlée to sit for a few minutes before serving.

# ISCHLER TOERTCHEN

*Yield: forty 2½-inch sandwich cookies*

*Many Eastern European desserts are defined by their use of jams, nuts or nut flours. This buttery cookie has all three. Originally gifted to me by a chef friend of Austrian descent (who claims that it came from a swanky resort in the town of Bad Ischl), this recipe is great for festive cookie cutters, and wrapped in a box and tied with a bow, the cookies make a wonderful holiday gift. My grandmother, whose family owned a tea and pastry shop in a small town called Vercez in what is now Serbia, made something very similar when I was growing up.*

### DOUGH

1 cup whole nuts of your choice

1 cup (8 ounces)
unsalted butter, softened

1 cup confectioners' sugar, sifted

2½ cups all-purpose flour

### FILLING

2 cups seedless jam or preserves,
store-bought or homemade
(see recipe on page 193)

**1.** Preheat the oven to 350°F. Toast the nuts on a rimmed sheet pan for 10 minutes, and then let cool. Grind the nuts in a food processor until they form a fine meal (see process on page 11). Leave the oven on for baking the cookies.

**2.** Line 4 rimmed sheet pans with parchment paper.

**3.** In the bowl of a stand mixer fitted with the paddle attachment (or using a hand mixer), beat the butter and confectioners' sugar on medium speed until soft and light, 2 to 3 minutes. Add the ground nuts, and mix on low for 30 seconds.

**4.** Remove the bowl from the mixer, and stir in the flour with a large rubber spatula, mixing until combined.

**5.** Scrape the dough out onto a lightly floured work surface and divide it into 3 pieces.

**6.** Flour one of the pieces of dough, and gently roll it out to a thickness of about ¼ inch. This dough is quite dry, but it bakes beautifully. You may have to press any cracks or crevices together, but that is okay.

**7.** Cut the dough with a large plain cookie cutter (2 inches in diameter) or a larger festive cookie cutter, and place the cutouts 1 inch apart in all directions on the prepared rimmed sheet pans.

**8.** Incorporate the scraps from the first piece of dough into the second piece, roll it out and cut more cookies. Repeat with the last piece of dough, incorporating any scraps before rolling. (Freezing the cookies on the rimmed sheet pans for 10 minutes before baking helps them to retain their shape, but is not necessary.)

When I felt like a change of pace, I grabbed confetti cake mix and a tub of strawberry frosting—a combo that might have trumped my sugary ice cream concoctions.

Flash forward a couple of decades and you will find a thirty-two-year-old me standing on top of a milk crate in front of a gas range in Ovenly's Red Hook commercial kitchen. There, with my sleeves rolled up high and clutching two ridiculously enormous whisks in my extra-long oven mitts, I would cook four giant pots of Salted Dark Chocolate Pudding (see recipe on page 184) at a time. This was how we filled our first thirty-gallon order for Steve's Craft Ice Cream, who swirled the pudding, along with bits of our stout cake, into their pints of ice cream. Without a fancy industrial steam kettle to rapidly cook large pudding batches, the gas range was our best—and only—option.

With the pots filled to maximum capacity, and ignoring the dictates of chemistry, I convinced myself that stirring faster would speed up the process (it does not). From time to time, hot splashes of dark pudding decorated my white apron. Every few minutes I would taste the steaming yet delicious pudding in order to monitor the progress and, as usual, would burn my mouth in the process. It was worth it. Erin stood close by, prepping for the next pudding shift. Our current estimate for completion time was eight hours.

Though the process was somewhat grueling, it was also strangely meditative and soothing. Who knew that observing the slow transformation of a thin liquid into a thick, velvety goop could be so therapeutic? Feeling pretty Zen, I looked up to see Erin adding cooled Salted Caramel Sauce (see recipe on page 190) to freshly made cream cheese buttercream, a blend that would be the topping for one of our stout cakes. I suddenly experienced that same giddy feeling I used to get as a kid.

The sauces and frostings that I once obsessed over in the grocery store aisles were being made in our very own (rented) kitchen! Better yet, our products were way better than what came out of the squeeze bottles and cardboard boxes of my childhood. This stuff was the real deal. And we were making truckloads of it with our own hands.

Erin and I make the fillings, frostings and sauces in this chapter regularly to enhance the flavors of our desserts, to finish and decorate them, or simply enjoy solo with a spoon. Yes, it is tempting to give in and buy a tub of frosting at the store rather than make it at home. However, developing the ability to make things from scratch, sometimes in just a few minutes, is a beautiful thing. We suspect that once you succeed with a few of these recipes, you'll never go back to those store-bought versions again. The outcome will be far more gratifying, and we guarantee that it won't last on a shelf for more than a day.

# BUTTERCREAM FROSTING BASE RECIPE

*Yield: enough for 20 cupcakes and one, two-layer 9-inch cake*

*When you finish making this simple yet classic buttercream, you'll want to dive into the resulting puffy, cloud-like frosting headfirst and then eat it all up. Once you master this recipe, you'll find yourself frosting everything you make, like us. Buttercream slathered over pancakes and maple syrup? Yes, please. Sandwiched between 2 cookies? The best. Smeared on toast for breakfast? We've tried it...and loved it.*

16 tablespoons
(1 cup, 8 ounces) cold
unsalted butter

7 cups confectioners' sugar
+ more for thickening

¼ to ½ cup heavy cream

**1.** Cut the cold butter into ½-inch pieces. Let it come to room temperature.

**2.** In the bowl of a stand mixer fitted with a paddle attachment, combine the butter, 3 cups of the confectioners' sugar and ¼ cup heavy cream, and mix on low until just incorporated. Then beat on medium-high until the mixture is creamy and ingredients are incorporated, about 1 minute. Scrape down the sides of the bowl with a rubber spatula.

**3.** Add more confectioners' sugar, 1 cup at a time, and mix on low until the frosting is thick but spreadable. Beat for 1 minute after each addition. You may not need to add all the remaining sugar. Once you have your desired consistency, scrape down the sides of the bowl.

**4.** Raise the speed to medium-high, and beat for 3 to 4 minutes, or until very light and fluffy. The buttercream should be thick but spreadable. If it is too thick, add a little more cream. If it is too thin, add a little more confectioners' sugar.

## Get Creative

· Chocolate Buttercream—Add ¼ cup high-quality American-process cocoa powder (like Valrhona) with the first addition of confectioners' sugar. For added flavor, melt ¼ cup milk chocolate chips, let the melted chocolate cool and then add it to the buttercream along with the cocoa.

· Vanilla Bean Buttercream—Scrape the vanilla bean caviar from a vanilla bean pod and add it to the buttercream during its final mix. For added oomph, also add 1 teaspoon of vanilla extract.

· Maraschino Cherry Buttercream—Add 3 to 4 table-spoons (to taste) all-natural maraschino cherry juice to the buttercream during its final mix. For added taste and texture, finely chop 5 or 6 maraschino cherries and beat them into the buttercream with the juice.

· Lemon Buttercream—Add the juice and zest of 1 lemon to the buttercream during its final mix.

· Honey Buttercream—Add ¼ cup honey with the first addition of confectioners' sugar. Honey makes buttercream looser, so you may need to add extra confectioners' sugar to find the right consistency.

## BUTTERCREAM PROCESS

01  Whip the butter until fluffy. Add in half the confectioners' sugar, and incorporate on low. Turn the machine off, add the remaining sugar and combine.

02  With the machine running on low, add the cream in a steady stream. Increase the speed to medium-high, and whip for 5 minutes, or until fluffy.

03  Turn the machine back to low, add any flavorings, and then return to high speed for 30 seconds to incorporate.

04  Ensure buttercream is thick but spreadable.

# POMEGRANATE BUTTERCREAM

*Yield: enough for one, two-layer 9-inch cake*

*Our culinary pursuits often find us roaming the import stores and market aisles, searching for new flavors to experiment with, which is exactly how we came across pomegranate molasses. Sweet and tart, it will make your mouth pucker with delight. We like to brighten up its deep natural brownish-burgundy color with a touch of natural red food coloring to play up the pink in the pomegranate.*

Buttercream Frosting Base Recipe
(see recipe on page 180)

2 tablespoons pomegranate molasses, or more to taste
(see Essential Tools & Ingredients on page 12)

Red or pink liquid food coloring, or gel (preferably all-natural)

**1.** Prepare the Buttercream Frosting Base Recipe, adding in the pomegranate molasses during the final mix.

**2.** Using a rubber spatula, scrape down the bottom of the bowl to incorporate any remaining pomegranate molasses. If the buttercream appears too thick, add in more cream, 1 tablespoon at a time. If it appears too thin, add more confectioners' sugar, 1 heaping tablespoon at a time. Taste the frosting. If you want a stronger flavor, add in more pomegranate molasses.

**3.** Add 3 to 4 drops red or pink food coloring into the bowl (or coat a toothpick with red or pink food coloring gel and mix it into the buttercream before beating), and mix on medium-high speed until the buttercream is uniformly pink. Add more coloring to reach the desired hue, as needed.

# DARK CHOCOLATE PUDDING BUTTERCREAM

*Yield: enough for one, two-layer 9-inch cake*

*If you're like Erin and me, and you have a couple bowls of pudding and buttercream sitting around next to each other, the two worlds are destined to collide. It was only a matter of time before our addictive pudding formed a beautiful union with our airy buttercream. If you make pudding as often as we do, this will be your go-to chocolate buttercream recipe.*

Buttercream Frosting Base Recipe (see recipe on page 180)

¾ cup Salted Dark Chocolate Pudding (see recipe on page 184)

½ cup dark Dutch-process cocoa powder (see Essential Tools & Ingredients on page 12)

¼ teaspoon salt

**1.** Prepare the Buttercream Frosting Base Recipe, substituting ¾ cup Salted Dark Chocolate Pudding for the cream.

**2.** Add the ½ cup dark Dutch-process cocoa powder and the salt with the first addition of confectioners' sugar. Mix on low until incorporated, and then follow the Buttercream Frosting Base Recipe.

**3.** Using a rubber spatula, scrape down the bottom of the bowl to incorporate any remaining pudding or cocoa powder. If the buttercream appears too thick, add more cream, 1 tablespoon at a time. If it appears too thin, add more confectioners' sugar, 1 heaping tablespoon at a time.

# SALTED CARAMEL CREAM CHEESE BUTTERCREAM

*Yield: enough for 20 cupcakes and one, two-layer 9-inch cake*

*We think adding cream cheese to anything sweet elevates the flavor to new levels. Subtly tart, this buttercream is the perfect partner for our Salted Caramel Sauce.*

Buttercream Frosting Base Recipe (see recipe on page 180)

½ cup Salted Caramel Sauce (see recipe on page 190)

½ cup (4 ounces) cream cheese, softened

**1.** Prepare the Buttercream Frosting Base Recipe, reducing the cream to 2 tablespoons to start and replacing the remaining cream with ½ cup Salted Caramel Sauce.

**2.** Once the Salted Caramel Sauce is fully incorporated into the buttercream and the buttercream is light and fluffy, add the cream cheese to the mixing bowl. Beat on medium-high speed for about 1 minute.

**3.** Using a rubber spatula, scrape down the bottom of the bowl to incorporate any remaining cream cheese. If the buttercream appears too thick, add more cream, 1 tablespoon at a time. If it appears too thin, add more confectioners' sugar, 1 heaping tablespoon at a time.

# SALTED DARK CHOCOLATE PUDDING

## *Yield: about 2 cups, 4 servings*

*I grew up eating pudding made from a powdered mix. I never touched those cold puddin' cups that my friends always had in their refrigerators. I preferred my pudding really warm, and only after it had developed a skin on top. If you're like me, this pudding should be eaten warm, or if you're like the rest of the world, once it's made, chill it and serve it topped with a spoonful of freshly whipped cream. It's rich and satisfying without being overly sweet. Plus, it trumps any store-bought puddin' cup out there.*

¼ cup + 1¾ cups whole milk

2½ tablespoons cornstarch

½ cup sugar

2 ounces (about ⅓ cup) dark chocolate, chopped*

3 tablespoons dark Dutch-process cocoa powder (see Essential Tools & Ingredients on page 9)

1 teaspoon vanilla extract

¾ teaspoon sea salt

*We prefer 60 percent cocoa content or highter

**1.** In a small bowl, whisk together the ¼ cup whole milk and the cornstarch until smooth. Set aside.

**2.** In a medium saucepan, combine the remaining 1¾ cups milk, sugar, dark chocolate, dark Dutch-process cocoa powder, vanilla extract and sea salt. Heat over medium-low heat, whisking, until the chocolate is melted.

**3.** Whisk the cornstarch mixture into the chocolate mixture until fully incorporated.

**4.** Reduce the heat to low, and continue to stir briskly with a wooden spoon or a heatproof spatula. The mixture will come to a simmer and will slowly begin to thicken.

**5.** Continue to cook for 1 to 2 minutes, or until the pudding coats the back of the spoon and slowly drips off. It will be thick and will just be starting to bubble.

**6.** Remove the pudding from the heat and pour into 4 serving ramekins or bowls. Let cool.

**7.** Cover with plastic wrap, refrigerate the pudding until it sets, and serve.

# CREAM CHEESE FILLING FOR CUPCAKES & MUFFINS

*Yield: enough for 16 muffins*

1 cup confectioners' sugar

3 tablespoons all-purpose flour

½ cup (4 ounces) cream cheese, softened

**1.** In the bowl of a stand mixer fitted with a paddle attachment (or using a hand mixer), mix together the confectioners' sugar and flour on low speed. Add the cream cheese, and beat on medium until smooth, about 1 minute.

# CREAM CHEESE TOPPING FOR CUPCAKES & MUFFINS

*Yield: enough for 16 muffins*

½ cup confectioners' sugar

¼ cup (2 ounces) cream cheese, softened

1 large egg, beaten and divided (only half is required, do not use other half)

**1.** In the bowl of a stand mixer fitted with a paddle attachment (or using a hand mixer), mix the confectioners' sugar on low. Add the cream cheese and beat on medium until smooth, about 1 minute. Add ½ of the beaten egg, and mix on medium-low until smooth.

# DARK CHOCOLATE GANACHE

*Yield: enough for 12 cupcakes or one single-layer 9-inch cake*

*Ganache is a beautiful thing: it's easy to make, yet it screams, "I'm fancy!" Besides being velvety and scrumptious, it's also really versatile. Use it as a glaze, frosting or filling. Smooth it on a cake to dress it up for any occasion, melt it and drizzle it over any dessert, or just mix it into peanut butter and eat it with a spoon for the ultimate late-night snack.*

8 ounces (about 1 cup) dark chocolate, coarsely chopped* (we use Callebaut 61 percent)

1 cup heavy cream

1 tablespoon butter (or use a neutral oil, like safflower)

Pinch of salt

*We prefer 60 percent cocoa content or highter*

**1.** Place the chocolate in a large heatproof bowl. Set aside.

**2.** Heat the cream in a medium saucepan over medium heat, and bring to a steady simmer.

**3.** Once the cream is simmering, pour it over the chocolate, ensuring that the chocolate is covered by the cream. Let it stand for 3 to 4 minutes, or until the chocolate has melted.

**4.** Add the butter to the chocolate mixture, and whisk until the mixture is completely smooth and shiny. Give it a final turn with a rubber spatula to ensure that no chocolate has settled at the bottom of the bowl. Add the salt and stir to combine.

**5.** If using the ganache as a glaze, immediately pour it onto the cake. For thicker ganache, set it aside to cool until it is spreadable but not hard. Once the ganache is spreadable, smooth it onto cakes or cupcakes.

*For Glazing a Cake:*

*Place a cake on a cardboard cake round (this makes it easily transferable from a work surface to a serving platter). Place the cake with the round on a wire rack with a rimmed sheet pan underneath it. While the ganache is still warm, pour a thin layer evenly over the cake, covering the cake completely. Smooth it with a spatula. Let the ganache cool completely before serving.*

*For Filling a Cake:*

*Allow the ganache to cool at room temperature for about 30 minutes, or until it is spreadable but not hard. Using an offset spatula, spread the ganache evenly on the bottom cake layer. Work from the center, spreading it out toward the edges of the cake and leaving about ½ inch of the cake visible at the outer edges. Place the top cake layer directly on top of the ganache.*

*For Cakes & Cupcakes:*

*Let the ganache cool for about 15 minutes. Transfer the bowl to the refrigerator to allow the ganache to set, and stir occasionally until it is spreadable but not hard. This should take no longer than 20 minutes. It should be easily spreadable but able to hold its shape.*

Get Creative

Try out different types of oils for the butter in the ganache to vary the flavor. Olive oil, coconut oil or hazelnut oil adds a subtle twist. Or omit the butter completely.

# SALTED CARAMEL SAUCE
## (Inspired by Spike)

*Yield: approximately 1½ cups*

*This is Erin's favorite caramel recipe, and it is the only one you will ever need. It can be used in cakes and buttercreams, spooned onto ice cream, mixed into pie fillings, drizzled onto pudding or eaten straight up with a spoon.*

1 cup heavy cream

¼ cup sugar

¼ cup (packed) light brown sugar

4 tablespoons (2 ounces) unsalted butter

3 tablespoons light corn syrup

¼ teaspoon salt

Caviar from ½ vanilla bean pod

**1.** Bring ½ cup of the cream, sugars, butter, corn syrup and salt to a boil in an uncovered 1½- to 2-quart, heavy-bottomed saucepan over medium-high heat. Once the sugars have dissolved, whisk the mixture a few times to combine. Continue to boil the mixture over medium-high heat, whisking occasionally, until deep dark tan bubbles form and until it has thickened and is paste-like.

**2.** When a candy thermometer reads 250°F (this takes about 5 minutes after the mixture reaches a boil), take the saucepan off the heat. (See note below if not using a thermometer.)

**3.** Pour in the remaining ½ cup cream and add the vanilla bean caviar, and whisk to incorporate. Be careful, as the mixture will bubble up and can splatter. Return the saucepan to low heat, and bring it to a low boil, whisking vigorously until no visible clumps remain and until the caramel sauce is smooth, about 45 seconds.

**4.** Immediately pour the hot caramel sauce into a jar or a heatproof bowl, and let it cool completely. Once it has cooled, cover it tightly and store it in the refrigerator or freezer. Reheat to use.

*You don't need a candy thermometer for this recipe as long as you use your nose and your eyes. The key is to take the caramel to a point just short of burning, so when the mixture begins to have a bit of a singed odor and when it looks paste-like and caramel-brown, quickly remove it from the heat.*

# CARAMEL PROCESS

01 Add all the ingredients minus ½ cup cream and vanilla bean caviar to a heavy-bottomed 2-quart saucepan.

02 Heat the mixture over medium-high heat. As the ingredients melt, whisk to combine.

03 Bring the mixture to a rolling boil. After about 5 minutes, large tan bubbles will form, and the caramel will be a dark golden brown.

04 Whisk vigorously to check the consistency. The caramel should be paste-like.

05 Remove the saucepan from the heat, and add the remaining ½ cup cream and vanilla bean caviar.

06 Return saucepan to low heat, bringing it to a low simmer and whisking vigorously.

07 Immediately pour the hot caramel sauce into a jar or a heatproof bowl, and let it cool completely. Once it has cooled, cover it tightly and store it in the refrigerator or freezer. Reheat in a microwave or saucepan to use.

# LEMON CURD

*Yield: approximately 1½ cups*

8 tablespoons (4 ounces)
cold unsalted butter

½ cup sugar

3 large egg yolks

2 tablespoons +
2 teaspoons lemon juice

2 tablespoons (packed) lemon zest

**1.** Cut the cold butter into ¼- to ½-inch cubes, and let it come to room temperature.

**2.** Place a small saucepan with about 1 inch of water over low heat and bring it to a simmer.

**3.** In a medium stainless-steel bowl, whisk together the sugar, egg yolks and lemon juice until well combined.

**4.** Place the bowl over the saucepan to create a double boiler. Simmer the sugar mixture, stirring constantly, until it thickens, about 10 minutes. The mixture is ready when it thickly coats the back of a spoon or when it reaches 160°F on a candy thermometer. When finished, it should resemble a thick hollandaise.

**5.** Immediately remove the bowl from the heat, and pour the mixture through a fine-mesh sieve into another bowl to remove any lumps.

**6.** Gradually whisk in the butter until all the butter has completely melted. Whisk in the lemon zest, and then let the lemon curd cool. Cover it immediately by pressing plastic wrap directly against the top of it to prevent it from forming a skin. The lemon curd will continue to thicken as it cools. Refrigerate it for at least 4 hours before using, and for up to 1 week.

# QUICK & EASY BLUEBERRY JAM

*Yield: approximately 1½ cups*

*What better accompaniment to a scone than butter and jam? Since we sell a lot of scones at Ovenly, we go through a lot of fixin's, as well. With all the fruit we have on hand, it was a no-brainer for us to start making our own jam. Don't be intimidated: all you have to do is throw everything into a large pot, heat and...wait.*

2 pounds fresh or frozen blueberries

¼ cup honey

**1.** Place the blueberries and honey in a medium saucepan. Heat over medium-high heat, stirring constantly to prevent burning, for 4 minutes.

**2.** After about 4 minutes, the blueberries will start to sweat. Turn the heat up to high, and stir until the liquid comes to a boil. Then reduce the heat to medium-low and allow the mixture to simmer for about 18 to 20 minutes, stirring every 3 to 4 minutes. The mixture thickens as it reduces.

**3.** For a juicier jam, reduce the cooking time by a few minutes. For a thicker consistency, cook the jam for the full 20 minutes. The longer you cook the jam, the thicker it will be.

**4.** Set the jam aside to cool and thicken fully. Store it in the refrigerator for up to 1 week.

**Get Creative**

· Substitute pitted plums, raspberries or cherries for the blueberries.

· Try using maple syrup instead of honey.

· Add a sprig of thyme or rosemary to the jam when it is heating on high, and then remove the sprig when the jam is done.

· When the heat is on high, add 2 tablespoons lemon or orange juice, red wine, brandy or your favorite sweet or boozy beverage.

# BAR SNACKS

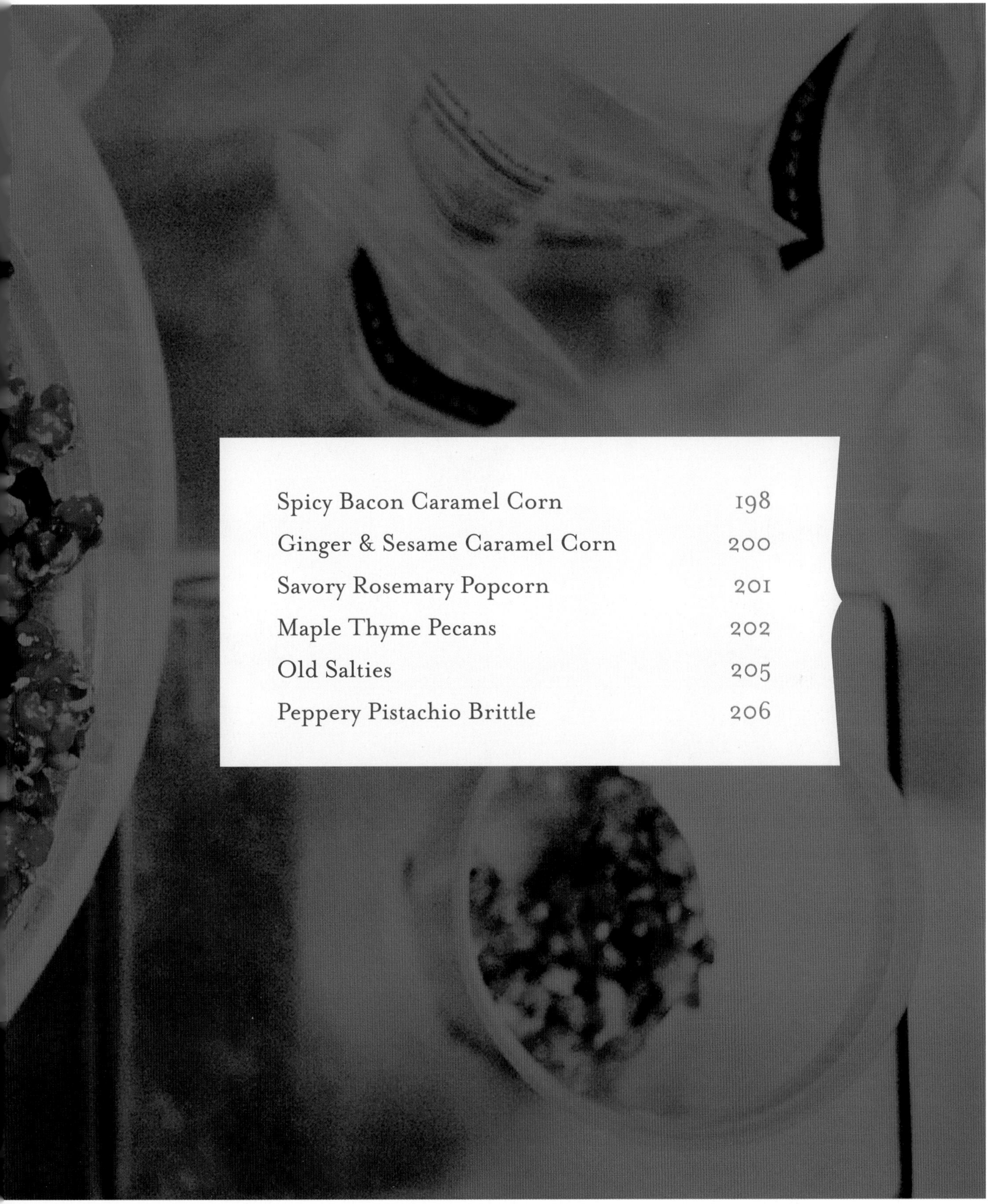

*Erin* ❖ The Ovenly bar snack was born one night—not surprisingly—at one of our favorite Brooklyn dives. Agatha and I were there after work, as usual, to debrief, decompress and sip bourbon, when we realized that neither of us had eaten lunch that day. We were kinda buzzed and really hungry.

As we eyeballed the sad-looking bags of potato chips and peanuts for sale behind the bar, our hearts sank. Soon we were in the middle of a heated discussion we'd had many times before: if alcohol and eating go hand in hand, why are most bar snacks so fucking bad? Pardon our French, but it's true. What the world needed, we decided, was a tastier booze-guzzling companion. Something you would want to shove into your mouth by the fistful. Something that enhanced that cold, delicious drink in our...er...your hand! Something that actually tasted good! Guided by our own grumbling stomachs, we started dreaming up the ideal munchie: it would be salty and spicy, and would deliver a bit of sweetness. We took notes and drank more booze.

The next day, we deciphered our scribbles, rolled up our sleeves and got to work. Within days, Ovenly's first signature bar snack—Spicy Bacon Caramel Corn (see recipe on page 198)—was born.

From there, we concocted an entire line of bar snacks, from unique caramel corns to kicked-up, herbaceous nuts. Pour yourself a drink and dive in.

# SPICY BACON CARAMEL CORN

### Yield: *approximately 3 cups*

*Though you don't have to pair this caramel corn with alcohol, we highly recommend it. There's just something about that salty-spicy-sweet goodness that begs for a cold brew or a shot of whiskey. We don't skimp with our pork, so this recipe is smoky and rich in flavor, with a touch of heat and sweet. We're partial to the hickory-smoked bacon from Benton's Smoky Mountain Country Hams in Tennessee (yes, they deliver), but any high-quality thick-cut bacon will do.*

Nonstick cooking spray or oil for coating the bowl, a rimmed sheet pan and metal spoons

½ cup lardons, or 10 slices regular thick-cut bacon (we love to use the bacon from Benton's Smoky Mountain Country Hams)

3 tablespoons bacon fat (from the bacon cooked in step 2)

½ cup popcorn kernels

1½ teaspoons baking soda

¼ to ¾ teaspoon cayenne pepper (or to taste)

3 cups sugar

¼ cup Brooklyn Brewery Pennant Ale (or any English ale)

¼ cup water

3 tablespoons unsalted butter

1½ tablespoons salt

**1.** Preheat the oven to 400°F. Spray 1 large mixing bowl, 1 rimmed sheet pan and 2 metal mixing spoons with nonstick cooking spray, or coat them with oil using a paper towel.

**2.** If using lardons, cut them into ¼-inch cubes, and bake them on an ungreased rimmed sheet pan for 30 minutes, or until very crisp. If using sliced, thick-cut bacon, bake it the same way.

**3.** Remove the lardons from the rimmed sheet pan with a slotted spoon or the bacon slices with tongs, and spread them on a paper towel–lined tray or plate. If using bacon slices, crumble the bacon once it has cooled.

**4.** Let the remaining bacon fat cool on the rimmed sheet pan, and then pour or spoon into an airtight container.

**5.** In a large pot with a lid or in a popcorn popper (Whirley Pop is our recommended brand), heat the bacon fat over medium-high heat. Add the popcorn kernels to the pot, cover with the lid and cook until all the kernels have popped, shaking constantly to prevent burning. If using a popper, follow the manufacturer's directions.

**6.** Transfer the popcorn to the prepared bowl, add the cooked lardons or crumbled bacon and mix.

**7.** In a small bowl, combine the baking soda and cayenne.

**8.** In a large heavy-bottomed pot, combine the sugar, ale, water, butter and salt. If available, attach a candy thermometer to the edge of the pot. Cook on high heat until the mixture boils. Let the mixture boil until the thermometer reaches 305°F or the caramel is a golden color. If the caramel does not reach 300°F, the caramel corn will turn out powdery, so we recommend using a candy thermometer. (You can get them at any grocery store or online.)

**9.** Once the caramel has a light caramel color or has reached 305°F, remove it from the heat and mix in the baking soda and cayenne. Stir for 30 seconds, or until all clumps of baking soda and cayenne have dissolved.

**10.** Immediately pour the caramel evenly over the popcorn in the bowl. Combine the caramel and the popcorn using the prepared spoons. Mix until the popcorn is well coated with the caramel.

**11.** Spread the caramel corn on the prepared rimmed sheet pan. Let it cool, and then break it into bite-size pieces by hand or with a dedicated chisel.

**12.** Store the caramel corn in an airtight container for up to 1 week.

### Get Creative

**Great uses for bacon fat**

Besides making Old Salties, there's a lot you can do with leftover bacon fat. Kept in the refrigerator in a sealed container, it lasts nearly forever and provides salty goodness to a variety of dishes.

· Reduce the butter in your favorite roasted nut recipe by half, and substitute bacon fat for the omitted half.

· Replace a quarter of the canola oil in our Cheddar Corn Muffin (see recipe on page 61) with melted and cooled bacon fat.

· Use it for popping any popcorn.

· Whip 1 stick butter with 2 tablespoons chilled bacon fat to make a porky spread for breads and muffins.

· Cook any of your breakfast favorites (eggs, pancakes, French toast, omelets) in bacon fat.

# GINGER & SESAME CARAMEL CORN

*Yield: about 3 cups*

*The healthy splash of beer in this caramel corn is the recipe's secret weapon—it offers just the right amount of tasty maltiness to balance out the punch of the ginger. We like Brooklyn Brewery's Sorachi Ace for its herby, summery flavor, but feel free to use any saison or farmhouse ale.*

Nonstick cooking spray or oil, for coating the bowl, rimmed sheet pans and metal spoons

2 tablespoons black sesame seeds

2 tablespoons white sesame seeds

3 tablespoons canola oil

½ cup popcorn kernels

2 teaspoons ground ginger

1½ teaspoons baking soda

3 cups sugar

¼ cup Brooklyn Brewery Sorachi Ace (or another saison or farmhouse ale)

¼ cup water

3 tablespoons unsalted butter

1 tablespoon salt

**1.** Preheat the oven to 350°F. Spray 1 large bowl, 1 rimmed sheet pan and 2 metal mixing spoons with nonstick cooking spray, or coat them with oil using a paper towel.

**2.** Bake both kinds of sesame seeds on the prepared rimmed sheet pan for 10 minutes, or until fragrant. Set aside.

**3.** In a large pot with a lid or in a popcorn popper (Whirley Pop is our recommended brand), heat the canola oil over medium-high heat. Add the popcorn kernels to the pot, cover with the lid and cook until all the kernels have popped, shaking constantly to prevent burning. If using a popper, follow the manufacturer's directions.

**4.** Transfer the popcorn to the prepared bowl. Add the toasted sesame seeds and mix. Set aside.

**5.** In a small bowl, mix together the ginger and baking soda. Set aside.

**6.** In a large heavy-bottomed pot, combine the sugar, ale, water, butter and salt. If available, attach a candy thermometer to the edge of the pot. Cook on high heat until the mixture boils. Let the mixture boil until the thermometer reaches 305°F or the caramel is a golden color. If the caramel does not reach 300°F, the caramel corn will turn out powdery, so we recommend using a candy thermometer. (You can get them at any grocery store or online.)

**7.** Immediately add the baking soda–ginger mixture to the caramel. With a mitted hand and using a long spoon, stir the caramel constantly with a rapid motion for about 30 seconds, or until the caramel takes on a deep orange color and is completely smooth and free of lumps.

**8.** Pour the caramel evenly over the popcorn and sesame seeds. Working quickly with a prepared metal spoon in each hand, combine the caramel and the popcorn. Mix well, until the popcorn is completely coated.

**9.** Spread the caramel corn in a single layer on the prepared rimmed sheet pan. Let it cool, and then break it into bite-size pieces by hand or with a dedicated chisel.

**10.** Store the caramel corn in an airtight container for up to 4 weeks.

# SAVORY ROSEMARY POPCORN

*Yield: 4 to 5 servings*

*This savory snack pairs the earthy crunch of toasted hazelnuts with the tangy, airy snap of deliciously seasoned popcorn. Unlike our other munchies, this one is best devoured within twenty-four hours, so make sure you have plenty of friends around to help you eat it immediately.*

¼ cup coarsely chopped raw hazelnuts

1 tablespoon unsalted butter

1 tablespoon coarsely chopped fresh rosemary

2 tablespoons canola oil

⅔ cup popcorn kernels

1 tablespoon hot paprika (preferably sharp Hungarian paprika)

Sea salt, to taste

**1.** Preheat the oven to 350°F.

**2.** Place the hazelnuts in a small baking pan. Bake for 10 to 12 minutes, or until lightly golden and fragrant. Set aside.

**3.** In a small saucepan over low heat, melt the butter. Add the rosemary, and cook for 2 minutes, or until fragrant. Remove from the heat.

**4.** In a large pot with a lid or in a popcorn popper (Whirley Pop is our recommended brand), heat the bacon fat over medium-high heat. Add the popcorn kernels to the pot, cover with the lid and cook until all the kernels have popped, shaking constantly to prevent burning. If using a popper, follow the manufacturer's directions.

**5.** Transfer the popcorn to a large bowl.

**6.** Drizzle the butter-rosemary mixture over the popcorn. Sprinkle with paprika and sea salt, and add the roasted hazelnuts. Gently toss to coat the popcorn and nuts evenly.

**7.** Serve the popcorn at once. It will keep in an airtight container for 1 day.

# MAPLE THYME PECANS

*Yield: 8 to 10 servings*

*These spiced-up pecans are great around the holidays—the blend of maple syrup, brown sugar and thyme makes us want to curl up next to a fireplace with a big bowl of the stuff. But the truth is that this treat is among our most versatile snacks—right at home at a cocktail party, paired with a glass of wine or a nibble of cheese; equally welcome as dessert, crumbled over your favorite ice cream.*

---

3 tablespoons (1½ ounces) unsalted butter, melted

2 pounds unsalted raw pecans

2 cups maple syrup (the darker, the better; we use Grade B)

½ cup (packed) light brown sugar

2 tablespoons + 2 teaspoons minced fresh thyme, or high-quality dried thyme

2 tablespoons + 2 teaspoons sea salt

1 tablespoon maple sugar

2 teaspoons cayenne pepper

½ teaspoon freshly cracked black pepper

**1.** Preheat the oven to 375°F. Line 2 rimmed sheet pans with parchment paper.

**2.** In a small saucepan or in a small, microwave-safe bowl in a microwave oven, melt the butter and set aside to cool.

**3.** In a large bowl, mix the cooled butter and all the remaining ingredients minus 1 teaspoon sea salt until well combined. Be sure to mix thoroughly in order to incorporate the wet ingredients, which may settle at the bottom of the bowl.

**4.** Spread the pecan mixture on the prepared rimmed sheet pans using a spatula. The pecans should be in an even layer on the rimmed sheet pans.

**5.** Bake for 18 to 20 minutes, stirring the pecans halfway through. The pecans are ready when they are lightly browned. Do not overbake.

**6.** Remove the pecans from the oven, and sprinkle them lightly with the remaining 1 teaspoon of sea salt. Let them cool completely on the rimmed sheet pans, and then scrape them from the parchment and separate any large clumps.

**7.** Store the pecans in an airtight container for up to 6 months.

# OLD SALTIES

*Yield: just over 1 pound, 6 to 7 servings*

*Sometimes a leftover spoonful of this or that will inspire an entirely new recipe, which is how these seriously addictive peanuts came to be. Scratching our heads over what to do with the leftover bacon fat from our Spicy Bacon Caramel Corn, we realized that we should be roasting nuts with it. What could be better with beer than a bacon-fat roasted peanut? The addition of Old Bay Seasoning and a splash of Worcestershire sauce sealed the deal.*

1 tablespoon unsalted butter

1 tablespoon bacon fat

1 tablespoon + 2¼ teaspoons Old Bay Seasoning

2 teaspoons freshly ground black pepper

1 teaspoon garlic powder

1 teaspoon salt

½ teaspoon red pepper flakes

1 pound shelled, unsalted raw peanuts

¼ cup Worcestershire sauce

**1.** Preheat the oven to 325°F.

**2.** Melt the butter and bacon fat in a small saucepan over low heat until combined, about 2 minutes. Remove from the heat and set aside. Bacon fat can burn rather quickly, so do not overcook.

**3.** In a small bowl, mix together the Old Bay Seasoning, pepper, garlic powder, salt and pepper flakes.

**4.** Add the peanuts to a large bowl, and pour the melted butter–bacon fat mixture over them. Add the Worcestershire sauce and the spice mixture. Using 2 large spoons, thoroughly mix the ingredients together until the peanuts are completely coated and there are no clumps of spice.

**5.** Spread the peanuts in a single layer on an ungreased rimmed sheet pan. Bake for 30 to 35 minutes, stirring the peanuts after 15 minutes and rotating the rimmed sheet pan to ensure even cooking. The peanuts are ready when they take on a golden-red color.

**6.** Store the peanuts in an airtight container for up to 6 months.

# PEPPERY PISTACHIO BRITTLE

*Yield: A lot!*

*This brittle isn't a traditional bar snack, but we like to pair it with wine or aperitifs. Though it is sugar based, the sesame and spices add savory undertones that play down the sweetness. Serve this brittle after dinner and in small pieces.*

Nonstick cooking spray or oil, for greasing the rimmed sheet pan

5 cups coarsely chopped, raw pistachio nuts

1 cup white sesame seeds

1 cup black sesame seeds

1 tablespoon + 1 teaspoon ground cinnamon

1 tablespoon + 1 teaspoon ground cumin

1 tablespoon salt

2 teaspoons freshly ground black pepper

9 cups sugar

**1.** Preheat the oven to 350°F. Grease a rimmed sheet pan with nonstick cooking spray, or coat it with oil using a paper towel.

**2.** Spread the pistachios, white sesame seeds and black sesame seeds on a second ungreased rimmed sheet pan, and bake until light golden and fragrant, 10 to 12 minutes.

**3.** Transfer the toasted nuts and seeds to a large bowl. Add the cinnamon, cumin, salt and pepper and mix well. Set aside.

**4.** In a large nonstick saucepan over medium heat, melt the sugar completely, stirring constantly. It will become a deep golden-brown color. Be careful not to burn it.

**5.** Once the sugar is just melted and beginning to turn brown, immediately add the nut mixture, reduce the heat to low and stir until smooth, about 3 minutes.

**6.** Pour the nut mixture evenly in a thin layer on the prepared sheet pan. Let it harden completely, about 30 minutes.

**7.** Break the brittle into 1- to 2-inch pieces with a dedicated chisel or by hand.

# ACKNOWLEDGMENTS

So many people have helped us to get where we are today. Here's just a small list of friends, family and colleagues to whom we owe our success.

Thank you:

Kathy, Stuart and Dan Patinkin, for scooping cookies and washing dishes on visits to New York. And for Dan's edits to (and insertions into and appearances in) this whole book.

Zdzislaw, Donna and Phillip Kulaga, for your unconditional (and ever-calming) love, patience and support.

Andy Dos Anjos, for being there from the very beginning, building Ovenly and for working for cookies (literally).

The Ovenly staff, for being the most wonderful, dedicated, hilarious and supportive employees on earth. And to Katie Ligon, for testing so many of our recipes.

Chuck and Mary Westphal, Randy Vittetoe, Bill Barnes and Vanessa Selbst—without you, Ovenly would not exist.

Winona Barton-Ballentine, photographer extraordinaire, for your creativity and commitment.

Katie Cancila, friend and food journalist, for helping us create the best proposal on the earth.

Brettne Bloom, of Kneerim, Williams & Bloom, for not giving up and for being the best agent anywhere.

Deb Brody, Becca Hunt and the rest of the Harlequin team, for having faith in us and in our company.

Jonathan Rubinstein, for your mentorship and partnership.

Heather Millstone, for being our first client. *Ever.*

Ben Hudson and the Brooklyn Brewery team, for serving and inspiring our snacks (and for all that beer).

Paulie Gee, for renting us your kitchen.

Tim Unich, of Gramercy Partners, for finding us our first home (and for sticking with us during all those lease negotiations).

Michael Fusco, graphic designer, for bringing our aesthetic to life.

Patrick Somerville, novelist and friend, for believing in our writing and convincing us this book was worthwhile.

Granny Ennis, wherever she is, for her culinary inspiration.

Stumptown Coffee Roasters, for being the best neighbors and friends.

Agatha's second family for life: Ashley Kreamer, Cara Cannella, Catherine Piercy, Cat Hartwell, Jesse Sposato, Jason Gilbert, John Rotrosen, Sara Francini and Winona Barton-Ballentine.

Erin's life support: Ali Hart, Mayme Hostetter, Bridget Ridenour, Sarah Nassauer, Nick Johnson, Sarah Abramson, Erin Mahoney, Ana Ortiz, Lindsay Booker, Julia Bloch and Dan Hockley.

Dr. Joseph Rumley, for lending us your apartment and the shirt off your back (literally).

The neighborhood and denizens of Greenpoint, for welcoming us to your community with open arms.

And to all our various friends, roommates and colleagues who believed in us, supported us and often-times worked for free to help us grow Ovenly.

Finally, thank you to all the artisans and crafters who provided their wares and services for this book:

Clam Lab

Courtshop

Roxy Coberly

Paula Greif

Niko, from Nars, makeup

Nina Lalli, stylist

Mociun

Mondays

The One Well

Crystal Saujon, personal stylist

Lady Soule, Design Director of Soft Wovens, Anthropologie

Tracy Reese

# INDEX

# ABOUT THE AUTHORS

*Erin Patinkin* ❖ spent her early years in Chicago, where she developed an obsession for Vienna Beef hot dogs (ketchup is sacrilege), Big League Chew and PBS cooking shows. At a young age, she saw past the Midwestern horrors of microwavable meals and fat-free cheese and relished the flavorful Polish and Austrian dishes her grandparents taught her to love, like matzo balls and poppy seed roll.

Before Ovenly, Erin worked as everything from an artist to a senior manager at a nonprofit feminist organization. All the while, she was honing her cooking skills, whipping up elaborate multicourse meals for friends and plotting her official move into the culinary world. The day she traded business casual for an apron and clogs was the best day of her life.

*Agatha Kulaga* ❖ grew up in Connecticut, where she was probably the only kid on her block eating traditional Polish dishes, like tripe soup, liverwurst and butter sandwiches and blood sausage. Some of her happiest childhood memories are of baking alongside her mother and grandmother, making Old World sweets, like apple cake, poppy-seed rolled cake and fat dessert dumplings.

Agatha spent over a decade working in restaurants before pursuing a career in psychology, but never stopped scheming about food: she experimented with novel flavor combinations, started a supper club and acted as her friends' personal pastry chef. She is grateful every day for the opportunity to grow Ovenly, which is rooted in her childhood love of Eastern European treats.

This is Erin and Agatha's first cookbook. In fact, it's their first book of any kind!